MAGIC
SEASON

Also by Wade Rouse

America's Boy

Confessions of a Prep School Mommy Handler

At Least in the City Someone Would Hear Me Scream:
Misadventures in Search of the Simple Life

It's All Relative: Two Families, Three Dogs, 34 Holidays, and
50 Boxes of Wine (A Memoir)

I'm Not the Biggest Bitch in This Relationship: Hilarious,
Heartwarming Tales About Man's Best Friend from America's
Favorite Humorists

Writing as Viola Shipman

The Charm Bracelet

The Hope Chest

The Recipe Box

The Summer Cottage

The Heirloom Garden

The Clover Girls

The Secret of Snow

Christmas Angels: A Holiday Novella

Christmas in Tinsel Tree Village: A Holiday Novella

MAGIC SEAS●N

A Son's Story

WADE ROUSE

HANOVER
SQUARE
PRESS

HANOVER
SQUARE
PRESS™

Recycling programs
for this product may
not exist in your area.

ISBN-13: 978-1-335-47517-6

Magic Season

Hanover Square Press
22 Adelaide St. West, 41st Floor
Toronto, Ontario M5H 4E3, Canada
HanoverSqPress.com
BookClubbish.com

Printed in U.S.A.

For my father

For the St. Louis Cardinals

And for every sports fan, father and son, parent and child, and soul who believes in hope, forgiveness and a win tomorrow

MAGIC
SEASON

"Love is the most important thing in the world, but baseball is pretty good, too."

—Yogi Berra

THE PREGAME

The game of baseball has been criticized in recent years for being too long. Too many substitutes, too many pitching changes, too many retreats from the batter's box, too many meetings on the mound, too many commercials. But it's actually a short journey from the first inning to the ninth, a couple of hours, and the outcome is often determined by little moments made from inning to inning, tiny decisions that decide the final score.

It is the same in life.

The last Cardinals game I watched with my dying father was filled with great hope and missed opportunities, just like life and the sport itself.

Our beloved St. Louis Cardinals were playing the hated Chicago Cubs in the National League Division Series. The Cards were down to their final game; my dad was down to his final weeks. We were both down to our final innings together.

Ironically, our relationship was a lot like the Cards–Cubs rivalry: intense, heated, bitter, filled with history and yet tinged with incredible admiration—and disgust—for the opponent.

We had little in common besides baseball. My father was an Ozarks man, born and bred, and I was a city boy, a liberal turncoat who up and ran from the place he was raised. He was an engineer; logic overruled emotion. I was a writer. You get the picture.

But I had a lot of the Ozarks in me, too, which can make a man as hard and unforgiving as the rocky terrain.

What did I have to forgive my father for?

How long do you have?

And yet I loved him.

So deeply, despite all he did and didn't do for me, that my heart still flutters and moves all about my chest to this day, just like a good knuckleball.

You will likely ask why I stuck by my father, or even gave him a second, third or fourth chance at all. So, I ask you this: Why do you stick by your favorite team, season after miserable season? It's because, no matter how pessimistic we've grown, no matter what we've long endured, we always believe that a miracle can happen, that a magical season will occur and obliterate all the bad memories that came before. A true fan believes in his heart that even a terrible team can turn into a great one.

Life, like being a baseball fan, relies on two things: hope and forgiveness.

The only thing I ever wanted was my father's approval. And I worked for it, yearned for it, through that final game, until his last breath.

Everything divided us. Except baseball.

Which was why I would take a seat next to him every time he patted the couch and the Cardinals were playing. I truly believed that, by the end of our final season together and that last game, the score would be different.

All I really wanted to do during our last game together was tell my father I loved him and forgave him. And all I wanted to hear was how much he loved me and how proud he was of me.

But, again, life and baseball really boil down to the simplest of things.

And those seemingly simple things would prove as difficult to come by as a big hit for the Cardinals in our last game together.

1ST INNING

GAME 4
St. Louis Cardinals-Chicago Cubs
National League Division Series

"Anything Can Happen"

October 2015

Before the start of every baseball game I ever watched with my dad—as soon as the National Anthem had ended and his hand was off his heart—he would say the same thing: "Anything can happen."

It was an astonishing statement of optimism from my eternally pessimistic father, who had pretty much hated the state of the world since his 1950s *Happy Days* life ended. But when the players took the field, the pitcher was warming up, the fans were buzzing, the sky was blue, the beer was cold and the game was scoreless, Ted Rouse was plumb near Walt Disney.

"Anything can happen."

"That's right," I say.

He is wearing the Cards cap I gave him after they won the 2011 World Series. It is still in pristine shape. The bill is unbroken and the shiny stickers are still attached, and my dying father looks as if he's trying to emulate today's urban youth.

I watch his head bob, and then he is asleep.

Suddenly, the Wrigley fans roar, and my dad jerks awake.

"Screw the Cubbies!" he yells as best he can at the TV.

He looks at me and nods as if to say, *I've still got enough life to roar back, too, son.*

We are sitting in the living room of the tiny home I had built for my nearly eighty-year-old father a few years ago. It was his wish to die at home. He hated his short-lived stint in assisted living.

"Doesn't play well with others," the home's administrator had told me as if my father was in preschool.

"I don't either," I told her.

At the time, assisted living was the only temporary solution. My father had been in a downward spiral since my mom died of cancer in 2009. His drinking had escalated, his health had declined, and he'd somehow turned into Ellen Burstyn in *Requiem for a Dream*, collecting Oxy from doctors all over the Ozarks. I'd found him nearly dead on a surprise visit, lying soiled in his own bed. While recovering in the hospital, my father not only detoxed but was tested for dementia. When the doctor asked him to draw a baseball diamond and he couldn't, I had to sprint to the hallway to hide my tears.

"You can't stay at home," I told him. "The bedroom and bath are upstairs, there's no railing on the stairway, the house is too big."

He refused to move near me, to leave the little town in which he'd lived his whole life. My father hated change. I was the king of surprises. I always teased him I should put "Refused to Change" on his gravestone.

"At least people will know where to find me," he'd say. "You, on the other hand…"

I look over at my father. His head is bobbing again, the Cards cap pecking the air like a duck's bill.

"I just want to die at home," my father told me in assisted living. "Die with dignity."

I remember a pain knifing through my heart at that moment because I knew that would be exactly what I'd want, too, at the end of my life.

So I helped him build a small, wheelchair-accessible home on the lot where my grandma and grampa had lived, and died. It was a big parcel of land set high on a hill that overlooked the main street into our tiny town as well as the rolling Ozarks hills leading out of it. From this vantage, my dad could see everything. It only seemed fitting that he could watch the town die as he did.

"We're both survivors, boy," my dad says to me out of the blue as the first inning of Game 4 is about to start. I lean closer to hear him. "That can be a good thing or a bad thing."

"Which is it, Dad?" I ask. "Good or bad?"

He smiles.

"Not up to me to decide anymore," he says. "What do you think?"

I look at him. "I don't know." I stop. "I think it's a good thing. Surviving means you've been tested. You're still alive for a reason."

A smile crosses his face. He shakes his head.

"You've always been an honest sum bitch," he says. "Too honest for your own good."

"Better to lie?" I ask.

"Sometimes," he says. "Makes life easier."

"For whom?" I ask.

"Turn the game up."

We listen to the National Anthem in silence.

Out of nowhere, my father reaches out and taps my arm. There are tears in his eyes.

"What is it, Dad?" I ask. "Are you okay?"

"No," he says. "I'm dying." He looks at me. "I don't know what's worse. Dying or living long enough to see the Cards lose to the Cubs."

He's always been funny. Something we have in common.

"They haven't lost yet," I say.

The game starts, but I can feel my father staring at me instead of the TV.

"Why are you still here?" he finally asks.

I know this is a bigger question than it sounds on the surface. He doesn't mean why did I extend my stay with him to watch this game but, literally, why am I still a part of his life?

"Because I love you."

I don't mean it to, but this comes out sounding like a question.

My father smiles.

Why am I still here? I think. *Guilt? Obligation?*

I glance at a photo on the wall of my family from my youth, the four of us in the old Rouse House, before death nearly swallowed my family whole as if the taste of grief was the most delicious thing in the world. My mother is looking at me in the photo in an adoring fashion, her hand in motion as if she's going to draw me closer to her. I hate platitudes, like when everyone says that dead people are saints, but my mother was as close to one as I will ever know. She was a hospice nurse who actually got what life was all about, what it meant to be here on this journey she used to call "as short as one blink of God's eye."

I think of my dad's question.

Why am I still here? For me, it comes down to the matter of being a good person. I look at my father and then at my mother. *No, scratch that. A better person.*

"My God," he says a second later as if he's been watching me. "You loved your mother. I've never seen two people love each other more in my life."

He makes it sound like a bad thing.

I stare at my father, as his eyes blink—once, twice—and then his head lolls to the side, and he is asleep again. *How can he be both so lucid and so loopy at the same time?*

I watch him snore. He is a very old man now, weak, so unlike the man I knew whose anger and rigidity and volatility and threats kept me quiet for too long.

"Are you a real man?" my father always asked. "Do you know what it's like to be a real man?"

What is a "real" man anyway? I always wondered.

And did I become the man I am today because of my father, or in spite of my father?

Spring 1972

"Anything can happen."

We both knew it was a lie, but—in the Ozarks—a dad had to teach his son to play ball, and a boy had to play ball. Period.

It was like baling hay, shooting a rabbit or gutting a fish. An Ozarks boy had to learn to do such things.

I wasn't your typical Ozarks boy. I would never be your stereotypical man.

I cried gutting my first fish, I puked shooting my first rabbit and I quit baling hay after my skin ripped, my shoulders blistered, and I was caught eyeing all the shirtless boys whose tanned torsos were drenched in sweat.

Baseball I couldn't get out of so easily.

"Why don't you go play ball with the other kids?" my dad would always ask me.

But we lived outside of town, on a dirt road in the woods, miles away from friends. Not that any of that would have mattered anyway. I preferred to be lost in a book, writing in my journal or going to the library. I preferred the kitchen over the playground, baking cookies with my grandma over kickball with schoolkids, wearing ascots and bow ties over overalls and sports uniforms.

None of this sat well with my father, who'd grown up a virtual Little Rascal, crawling in ditches, rummaging in trash cans, playing stick ball in the street. My father was a little man with a big presence. Born a tadpole, Ted Rouse never grew to be more than five foot five and a buck forty when wet. He tried to play football in high school as if he were twice that big, though, before breaking bones more easily than he broke bread every Sunday. He eventually settled on tennis, where he still threw himself around the court with abandon. He didn't learn. He went on to box in college and was always showing off the bend in his oft-broken nose as a point of pride.

If an illustrator were to have drawn my father as a character in a comic strip—the old-school kind that used to appear in color in the Sunday paper when he and I were kids, the ones I traced onto Play-Doh—he would have been a mix of Li'l Abner and Andy Capp. He deemed himself a paragon of innocence in a dark and cynical world, his excuse and escape drinking and having fun.

When my dad asked me to play T-ball, I refused. When he wanted me to play flag football, I said no. When he drove me to play catch with some of the guys he hunted with, I trembled so terribly, one of the hunters said I reminded him of a scared rabbit in the crosshairs of his scope.

"Those are the rabbits that need to be shot," he said to me. "They ain't gonna make it long in the world anyway."

For me not to play sports was an affront, not only to our

little town's code of life but also to my father, his world and expectations. It mattered only that I fit the mold that had been created for Midwestern boys in rural America in the 1970s.

Why didn't he force my brother, Todd, to play sports? Because Todd checked most of the other boxes on the rural father-son checklist: Avid hunter, with guns and bows. Tinkerer of engines. Tree climber. Mud-pie maker. Boot wearer. Skoal chewer.

So, without asking, my father arrived home one night to announce that he'd signed me up to play summer Little League. I was furious.

"You know I can't play," I protested.

"You're not trying," he said.

I begged my mom, who took my side on most things.

"Give it one more try," she said. "Your father will teach you. Right, Ted?"

Quid pro quo before I even knew what that meant.

A gulp of his beer. A moment of silence. A nod.

My mother's checkmate meant my father would be forced to spend time with me.

Most days, after the school bus would let me out, I would walk the mile home on our dirt road. I'd grab a snack— a Pop-Tart, a bowl of Count Chocula, a Little Debbie— and flip on the TV. I'd watch reruns of *The Brady Bunch*, *Batman*, *Gilligan's Island*, *I Dream of Jeannie* and *The Munsters* until my father came home. He'd immediately grab a beer, two gloves and a baseball, flip off the TV and urge me into the backyard.

To say I was not an athletic child would be like saying

Paul Lynde was not John Wayne. My body—as soft and spongy as a Twinkie—was not agile and lithe like the boys in my class. My mind and imagination were my strengths. My body was my liability. As a boy from the Ozarks, you strived for the reverse.

"First things first—hold your glove like this," my father would tell me. "Punch the leather. Feel it on your hand. Make it an extension of your arm. It's part of you."

My father may have been small in stature, but he seemed like a giant to me. Don't all dads seem that way to their sons? His voice was rumbly and rocky, and it reverberated like a bad muffler on an old pickup bumping along a dirt road.

"Pick up the ball, boy!"

To say I threw like a girl would misrepresent every girl in the world because they threw better than me. I threw as if my arm were made of a Slinky.

"Goddamn it, son!" my father yelled. "What in the Sam Hill is wrong with you?"

Everything was wrong with me. I had hair like Farrah and a body like a VW. My father knew it. Everyone knew it but ignored it.

My father grabbed the baseball and whipped it directly at my body. I ducked, and the ball went flying into the bramble of woods that ringed our home.

"Get it, boy!" my dad yelled.

I raced into the woods, my shirt and skin snagging on the thorns of the blackberry vines that grew wild, and returned, drenched in the Ozarks humidity.

My father walked over and adjusted my arm and body just so.

"Again," he'd say.

My father was a chemical engineer who believed that life was an equation to be worked through. Everything was black-and-white. But I was comprised of all emotion. I cried. I talked to rabbits. I admired the beauty of the cotton-candy clouds at sunset. I was an equation my father could never solve.

We continued this charade for months. Every practice session ended as a standoff between the two of us. My father would rage. I would cry.

Most evenings both of us mercifully gave up when the sun slunk behind the oaks. My father would retreat into the house, grab another beer and turn on the radio to the St. Louis Cardinals game. Jack Buck's voice was a mediator in our home. His presence meant that my father and I would not have to confront one another as long as the Cardinals were playing. And it was through Mr. Buck that I would become a student and fan of the game.

Of course, my playing career was short-lived, but it culminated in an infamous flameout. Unknowingly, when my father had signed me up to play Little League, he didn't realize the team sponsor was Mary Kay. My uniform was bright pink, and it was the very first thing about baseball that I absolutely adored. My father was aghast.

"What's happened to America?" he asked. "Boys in pink!"

I had been designated the fourth outfielder, a position that doesn't even exist in real baseball, but *everyone* on the team played in every game in our Little League since the town had so few kids. I was placed in deep center field, where I stood as lifeless as a gay flamingo.

I struck out nearly every time at bat. Once I hit a double that went all the way to the fence—it should have been ruled as two errors—but I only made it to first base. I prayed that no balls would ever be hit my way, but, of course, most were. My agility was terrible, but my hand-eye coordination was even worse. I didn't actually ever drop a fly ball. I couldn't even judge where the fly balls were going. Things did not come naturally. Part of it was my weight. I was shaped more like a cartoon sponge than an athlete. Part of it was my eyesight. I was nearly blind, but my poor vision would largely go undiagnosed for a few more years, despite the fact I tripped over the ottoman more than Dick Van Dyke. Most of it, though, was simply because I didn't naturally fit into the roughhousing of boys, the tough talk, the spitting, the punching of shoulders.

But my brief Little League experience defined my life in many ways. I learned to see the funny in everything. I learned that irony can be found in the most unlikely of places, even the Ozarks.

What would I do when the entire team surrounded me in the parking lot after I blew another game striking out four times or losing a ball in the sun yet again? I'd point at a kid with a mole on his face and say, "I couldn't see because Holy Moly here was blinding me!" The boys would laugh and punch the other kid instead of me. I ended up being the one invited to go along because I was good for a laugh.

I may have felt guilty about throwing other kids under the bus, but, in the Ozarks, it was all about self-preservation.

I also saw the way laughter brightened the world. My grandma would sit in her kitchen, bone-tired after an exhausting week of stitching overalls at a local factory. Her back would be as bent and broken as a peony stem, but when she'd read acclaimed humorist Erma Bombeck's column, "At Wit's End," in the local paper, she would smile, then laugh, and I could see her entire disposition brighten.

Humor would become not only my defense mechanism but also a way to make sense of the world around me.

But mostly I only wanted to make one person laugh. I only worried about one person's opinion of me. In my heart, I believed that my father didn't particularly like me. Despite coaching me in the backyard and signing me up to play, he didn't show for my very first baseball game. He didn't show for any of my games. When I asked him, he said he had to work late, but he never worked late. When I would get home, angry, slamming my glove onto the dinette set, I would go to the trash compactor and count the empty beer cans. He had gotten home on time.

So, I quit baseball.

I switched to things I enjoyed—despite my father's tantrums. I joined the band and played trombone. I was very good, getting the highest marks—a rating of 1, or Superior—at state instrumental competitions, as well as scholarships to college. I played in jazz band. I marched in parades. I had the leads in high school theatrical productions. I was a student council officer and top ten in my class. I was the first boy to ever be elected an officer in the Future Home-makers of America.

I did things my way, just like Frank Sinatra.

But the only thing I ever wanted was to make my parents happy. To hear my father scream, "That's my kid right there!" To hear "I love you!" before bed.

Being different, I yearned for acceptance. I only wanted to be liked and loved.

My family had a large family reunion at our cabin one summer. Everyone came, including great-aunts from California and distant cousins I'd never met. We all gathered on the rocky beach for photos, a throng of Rouses dressed in swimsuits and jean shorts clumped in front of the creek. As we began to break apart, each family posed for their own photo. When it came time for ours, the four of us smiled, my mother's arms wrapped around both her sons.

"Let me get one of you and the boys, Ted," I can remember my mom saying. "That never happens."

We posed, and my mother took photos.

"Now just you and Wade," my mom said.

"You got enough, Geraldine!" my dad said.

I stood there, and—as if in slow motion—my father looked at me and walked away.

My mother managed to get one picture: me, looking at my father, my face near tears, and the back of my father's leg, foot in motion, walking away from me.

October 2015

My father wakes with a start. The top of the first is underway. It's hard to tell how quickly he is failing, but his face and body are more bloated. He can no longer move without assistance. Often, he hallucinates. He has conversations with his dead parents. He calls for my mom in the kitchen. He talks about things that happened thirty years ago as if they are happening now. I receive anywhere between twenty and fifty phone calls a day from him. Each time he sounds like a child who gets separated from his parents in a mall. Some of the time he asks when I'm coming to see him. Most of the time, he tells me of his dreams, something he has never done in his life.

He has lots of dreams. He dreams that his parents, my brother, or my mom call to tell him they're waiting for him on the outskirts of town. He drives to see them, they have a picnic—my grampa's fried chicken, my mom's potato salad, my grandma's blueberry pie, a cooler full of ice-cold beer—and they tell him, "It's almost time."

"Time for what?" he asks.

And then a whip-poor-will will call—*Whip-poor-will! Whip-poor-will! Whip-poor-will!*—and he wakes up.

But the dream he says he has most often is the two of us watching a ballgame together.

"Like we always have," he says.

My dad looks at me, then the TV and slowly tries to grasp where he is.

"Hi, Dad," I say.

"Damn commercials," he says. "I don't like the feel of this game already. Not at all."

"Anything can happen," I say.

He looks at me and tugs on the bill of his cap. "Damn optimist," he says.

There's my dad, I think. I can still see him buried beneath the ravages of aging, screaming to be heard.

"Hey," I say. "I'm just repeating what you've always said."

"But you always believed it."

I duck my head, feeling a mix of pride and shame.

Eventually, my father and I gave up on his attempts to make me a baseball player. But something grew out of that failure. My father couldn't teach me baseball, I couldn't learn to play, but we listened to every game together, spring through fall. The gay kid and the Ozarks man listened, watched and attended thousands of Cardinals games together.

At first, my interest was driven solely by my desire to bridge the gap with my father. If I did something he liked, he might like me more.

And when I expressed interest, my dad taught me how to score a game.

"It's like a mathematical formula, you see?" my dad would say. "Game is like chess. One move at a time."

Slowly, I could see, in real time, how a pitcher performed, or how defensively sound a team was.

I began to score my own cards during a game. I started a journal, marking the day-by-day win-loss standings of the Cardinals, noting the winning or losing pitcher, their ERA, how many games ahead or behind the Cards were during the season.

My father and I learned to talk only of the Cardinals: Al "the Mad Hungarian" Hrabosky, Lou Brock, Bake Mc-Bride, Bob Forsch became a way for us to connect and spend time together.

We never talked about my life. I longed to be a writer, which was not something that my father could easily quantify. An engineer, a doctor, a lawyer, a salesman—these were jobs that could be said with pride.

Over time, however, I began to genuinely love the game of baseball. It provided moments of escape, and solace, in my life. I admired the dueling simplicity and complexity of the game: each pitch, each at bat, each move determined the outcome. It seemed so easy on the surface, but navigating a game was filled with important decisions and crucial moments.

I admired the skill of players being able to do something I couldn't do, just as much as I admired authors. The talent, dedication and resilience it took to be successful lodged in my soul.

I also began to understand the importance of sports. I could root for something bigger than me, my father, my little town. I could escape into another world.

But mostly I actually began to enjoy spending time with my father. In the quiet moments, he would tell me of his day, his job, his childhood. I began to connect the dots, understand how he became the man he did.

And when he'd pat the end of the couch, I finally knew it wasn't meant for the dog to come curl up next to him.

The gesture was meant for me to join him.

My father reaches over from his recliner and pats the couch as best he can, and I scooch down an inch or two, even though I am already as close to the arm as I can be.

I look over at him. He is staring at me. He is going to open up to me, I think. Tell me he's proud of me.

"What is it, Dad?"

"Did you ever hear the joke about Saddam Hussein?"

I shake my head.

"You know, they shouldn't have assassinated Saddam, don't you?" he asks.

"What should they have done?"

"Locked him in a jail cell with a hundred faggots," he laughs. "They would have taught him a lesson. That would have been punishment enough."

He waits for my reaction. I can feel the rage build, my heart race, the bile in my throat. I squelch it all and look at him.

He glares at me, waiting for a sign of weakness. I refuse to show him a single one.

I stand. He tries out of reflex to stand, or move, or reach for me, I don't know, but he can no longer function on his own. Now it's me who can walk out of a room.

"I'm going to bed," I say, even though it's only late afternoon.

"What about me?"

"That's why we have round-the-clock care," I say. "I can call Sue to come in. She can be here in a half hour."

"I don't want Sue," he says. "I want you."

That's what I always wanted, too, I don't say.

"Good night, Dad."

In the spare room I walk past my husband, Gary, cover my head in the pillow and scream. I'm caught in an Ozarks cycle. Run, return, actually believe for once that things will change, that my support, love and decisions have actually made a difference. I move the pillow and gasp for breath, the Ozarks air sticky on my face. My father does not believe in air-conditioning. I grew up without it.

"Waste a money!" he always said. "Makes a man weak!"

So I spent my childhood summers in a home with few windows that opened and only an attic fan to suck in humid air. I became so conditioned to living in intolerable heat that I can barely deal with AC. I shake. I tremble. I turn it off.

"Boy!" my dad yells.

I hear my father moan from the living room. It's an act, a cry for attention, a call for me to come. It sounds horrible, I know, but it's the truth.

Dementia is a terrible disease. We only think that it robs the mind, but before it does, it reveals everything about the person, the truths and ugliness and, yes, even the beauty.

My mom always knew it would come down to the two of us, me versus my father. "You and your father have so much unfinished business," she once told me. "And you need to conclude it without a mediator. You need to finish all this on your own terms." It was as though she planned her exit early so we would have to duke it out, face off, and see who survives.

Cubs versus Cards.

My father's words ring in my ears.

We're both survivors, boy. That can be a good thing or a bad thing.

Even as I near fifty, I often still don't know which one it is despite my optimism.

My father yells, and I can't take it.

"Don't," Gary says.

I stop and look at him.

"Why do you do this to yourself?"

I shrug my shoulders.

"You're a good man, Wade Rouse," he says.

"Am I?" I ask.

I walk back into the living room. A smile emerges on my father's face. He pats the couch again, and I take a seat.

Suddenly, tears are running down his face. Dementia has made him vulnerable for the first time in his life. He's like a child. And I'm actually thankful for that. He does want me here, even if he can't say it. At least I can see it now. It's tangible.

"You came back?"

It is both question and statement.

"We still have an entire game to play," I finally say. "Anything can happen."

My father shakes his head at me.

"What'd Yogi Berra say?" I ask. "Remember?"

I note a flicker of recognition in my father's eyes, but he can't put the words together.

"It ain't over till it's over," I say.

"Damn optimist," my father says.

"Cards are up to bat," I say.

Stephen Piscotty hits a homerun. 2-0 Cards.

"Screw the Cubbies!" my dad roars.

He lifts his hand weakly, and I high-five it.

You never know which way the ball will bounce, I think.

I am either way too weak or way too strong, but I can't give up on my Cardinals, or my father. It's a gift or curse, this belief that things will turn out better than expected, this hope that a miracle will occur before the game ends. It's gotten me this far in life. I'm a sarcastic optimist who can cut someone down to size and yet cry at a dog food commercial. Either I'm a masochist or an optimist. It's why I put a knife to my wrist and stopped. It's why I write books that honor memories and traditions.

It's why I'm here right now.

Because I believe that life is too short, too valuable, too beautiful to squander, and that it can change on a dime just like a game.

My father may not have shown up, but I always will.

We sit in silence and listen to the rest of the first inning, enjoying the one thing we have in common: a love of baseball and the St. Louis Cardinals.

And while that may not have been enough for us to forge a close relationship, at least it was enough to unite us for a few hours every year for decades.

And, as I settle into my twilight, I've come to realize this is still more than most people ever get.

Anything can happen, I think.

2ND INNING

"Always Develop the Farm System"

October 2015

My father loves Cards infielder Matt Carpenter. He is a product of the Cardinals farm system, meaning he was drafted by St. Louis and learned, what is known in Missouri, as the Cardinals Way.

It sounds a bit pretentious—the Cardinals Way—and it likely is. But, in my heart, there is no other way.

In 1919, Branch Rickey, then manager of the St. Louis Cardinals, devised what came to be known as the "farm system," the minor leagues that now groom and develop talent for the Big Leagues. As the price of established players increased, the Cardinals began "growing" their own, signing hundreds of high-school boys. As a result, they established their own player development machine, which would fuel them—after struggling for many decades—to their first World Series Championship in 1926. That began a twenty-one-season run in which St. Louis captured nine National League pennants and six World Series championships.

Baseball being a copycat sport, other teams followed suit.

My friends who love the Cubs, the Brewers or the Dodgers, often scoff at the Cardinals Way, but I point to history. My father taught me all about that.

He believed in the fundamentals of sound baseball, just like the Cardinals. You hit to get on base, not to homer every time, you don't strike out, you play solid defense, you bunt to move a player up a base instead of swinging for your own glory and you put the ball in play with a runner on third.

"All the little things that add up to determine the outcome of the game," my father told me. "All the little things that make the difference in the end."

This was his philosophy in life, too. There was a way to play it, a rulebook already established, a farm system in place, and you don't change it. You just play by those rules the best way you can.

My dad is still rambling about Matt Carpenter's single in the first inning—not Piscotty's homerun that just gave the Cards the lead. "He knows the Cardinal Way," my dad keeps repeating. "Not flashy. Does it the right way. All the little things. Not the star. Not the big paycheck. Earns it."

Earns it.

I nod robotically because I've heard this all my life.

That's because instead of the Cardinals Way, we had the Rouse Rules.

My dad developed his own farm system. He was founder, CEO and president, and if you didn't play by his rules, you weren't a part of the game.

My father built our family home—an Arkansas stone home that seemed to rise from the earth like one of the

Ozarks bluffs—working on it for years himself in order to save as much money as possible.

The Rouse House, he called it. It would become my sanctuary and prison.

The first rule of the Rouse House was that it was my father's house. His house, his mortgage, his rules.

He woke predawn and made his coffee, which was weaker than tea. You could actually see through it. My dad always bought the giant tubs of the cheapest coffee he could find, and he would use it sparingly. The heat was always set at fifty-eight degrees, even in the dead of winter. Appliances were unplugged. Lights had to be turned off when you walked out of a room. We had a washer that leaked, but my father duct-taped it together and stacked towels underneath it for well over a decade rather than pay someone else to repair it.

But the biggest Rouse House rule was that you didn't spend the money you earned. You saved it. You invested it. It was not real. It disappeared into the ether, into the farm system, only to be utilized when it had reached its ultimate potential.

And yet my father talked about money nonstop: How much he made. How much he saved. How well a stock was doing. How much his portfolio would be worth when he was sixty-five.

Growing up, I always pictured my father's money as a pot of gold at the end of the rainbow. It was mythical. I envisioned piles of money, gleaming in the sun, always out of reach. In many ways, we lived modestly: my brother wore hand-me-downs, my parents drove old cars, we used old tires as garden decor. Despite his education and job, my dad was a product of his environment. He liked to act as if we were not at all different from our neighbors who dwelled in trailers that sat on concrete blocks in the hollers just down the dirt road from us.

He was also a product of his past. My father was born in the midst of the Great Depression, and the impact that had on him and my grandparents never diminished. My grandma Rouse saved tinfoil as if it were actual silver—it was folded and stacked in every single kitchen cabinet—and she used sugar and eggs as carefully as if they were real saffron. My grandma made most of my clothes, and when they got worn, they were patched and re-patched. Kids jokingly called me "hobo" when I was little. I spent summers at a log cabin with my grandma and grampa Rouse. We had no phone, no TV, no indoor bathroom, no heat and barely enough food to eat, although my grandfather had worked his way up to district manager at the local electric company. He made a nice living and had a wonderful home, but the economic feeling was always one of impending doom.

"We could lose what we have at any time," my dad and grampa said every single day. "Save every nickel. Watch every dime. Pick up a penny or button if you see it on the ground."

And yet those summers with my grandparents were magical. I learned that you didn't need much to truly feel rich. Ostentatiousness was a sign of ego; being humble was a reflection of God. Bathing in the creek was more grand than taking a dip in any claw-foot tub.

My other grandparents were truly working poor. My grandma Shipman was a seamstress who stitched overalls at a local factory. She never learned to drive, walking to work every day, her body a reflection of her long hours. By the end of her life, she resembled a comma, and the knuckles on her hands were as round and red as radish. The story goes that my grandma and grampa had an old crock in their garage. Whenever they had spare change—a dime here, a quarter there—they would toss it in. Over time, the crock got full, so they loaded it in the back of their pickup and hauled it to the local community bank, where they started a college fund for my mother. She would become the first in our family to graduate college. That change changed the life of my mother and our entire family.

I used to spend inordinate amounts of time with my grandmothers. I would watch them pull recipe cards from their recipe boxes and make pies and crusts from a few simple ingredients, better desserts than I've even had at Michelin-starred restaurants.

I watched them make beautiful quilts from scraps, or make a blouse look new again by finding just the right buttons from their button jars.

"Look at this beautiful button, Wade," my grandmas would say. "All forgotten. All with a story. All from someone and somewhere. These hold value, these things that just get tossed aside. Never forget that."

Every morning at dawn after making his coffee, my father would stomp by the bedrooms of me and my brother as if an entire marching band was parading around the house. As soon as the first cup was in his system, my father would stomp back up the stairs bellowing the lyrics to a song he used to sing while marching in formation in the army, a song I later learned was from the Broadway musical *Wildcat*, from which he must have altered the words:

> *Hey, look me over*
> *Lend me an air*
> *I'm in the clover*
> *Clear up to here…!*

He would stop at our rooms, and if he didn't hear us rumbling awake, he would beat on our doors and yell, "Rise and shine! Time to earn a dime!"

That meant it was time for us to wake up, no matter if it were a school day or the weekend. My mom often worked nights at the local hospital, returning home in time to make my brother and I breakfast and check on our homework. I used to joke that I wanted to work nights so that, like her, I could sleep, uninterrupted, for seven hours when my dad was gone and the Rouse House was blessedly empty and blissfully quiet.

I worked hard growing up. During the school year, I delivered *Grit*—a former weekly newspaper popular in rural America—at dawn. A chunk of those summers with my grandparents was spent doing projects for them and their neighbors. I helped repair mortar in log cabins, I kept the stepping-stones from accumulating moss, I cleaned debris from beaches. As I grew older, I mowed lawns. In high school and college, I worked at the local newspaper, first assisting with odd jobs and then as an intern and reporter.

In college, I worked at the mall, first at Sears and then at a knife kiosk, yearning to work at the cooler stores, like Chess King, Orange Julius, or Spencer's.

But I didn't get a cent of any of the money I earned. My paychecks and my crumpled dollars went directly to my father. He was, in Cardinals terms, my Branch Rickey. In my terms, my father was my financial pimp.

All of my money was invested, just like his was. My father purchased stocks, bought me CDs and placed money into my college fund. There was no money for gas, or pizza on Fridays, or weekends at the mall. Sometimes my mom and grandmas snuck me money, on the down-low, as if I were a spy. I would find five dollars in my wallet from my mom, or my grandma would leave an envelope in one of my schoolbooks with a ten. They didn't want my dad to know. I would be so overwhelmed by the generosity that I wanted to run out and spend it immediately. But I couldn't. I would squirrel it away for later, knowing I might need it for an emergency. On the rare occasion a friend would coerce me into buying a gift for myself, I would immediately feel guilty and return home and hide it in the closet, never to use it because it was too special, like the candles my mother received from friends that sat in a cabinet, melting and unused, because spontaneous presents were so rare and so precious.

On my sixteenth birthday, my parents bought me my first car. When I got home from school, a 1976 Mercury Cougar—as big and sturdy as a tank—was sitting in the driveway. I was ecstatic. I wasn't used to many—much less such extravagant—gifts. In fact, our family never traveled.

Anywhere. Our biggest trips were to the cabin, or we'd throw our clothes into garbage bags, which served as our luggage, and my dad would drive us around Old Route 66 for a night on the road where we'd stay at the kookiest motels, ones on spots where UFOs had supposedly landed and beds that vibrated for a quarter.

"Thank you! Thank you! Thank you!" I yelled.

"We used your money to buy this," my father said. "I cashed in one of your CDs. You don't owe a penny on it, except for insurance, which you will pay yourself."

"It's not a gift?" I asked.

"Oh, it is, son," my father said. "A practical gift that you earned. This shows you the power of money when it's invested and not squandered."

Years later, when I needed to replace the Cougar, my father actually bought a vehicle for me outright, using his own money this time, as a financial lesson.

When he discovered the interest rate that I was being offered, he told the salesman, "I can give my son a better interest rate than you can." And he did.

My father made his own payment coupon books, which he sent me every few months. If I didn't pay on time, I was assessed interest. If I balked, as I did one time because I wanted to buy a new suit for work, my father threatened legal action if I missed a payment. So I paid every month. Early. Plus extra, in order to pay off the loan as quickly as possible.

I drove those cars into the ground. They rarely required any maintenance or repair. The trade-in values were always strong. I finally realized that my father was not only trying to teach me a powerful financial lesson, he was actually demonstrating a powerful expression of love. For a man who spent words like he spent money, he was using the only vocabulary he had to let me know how much he cared. He was trying to protect me from all of the pain his elders had endured: depression, war, poverty.

They were cars, yes, but they were actually vehicles of emotion.

When I bought my first home in St. Louis, I felt like I was a master of the game. I looked at hundreds of homes. I knew the up-and-coming neighborhoods. I had a feel for design. I settled on a two-bedroom, one-bath shingled bungalow in a good suburb that was adjacent to some of St. Louis's priciest neighborhoods. The home was adorable: a former country house from the early 1900s when the wealthy took carriages out of the city for fresh air. It had a wide front porch, a private backyard, a detached two-car garage, a windowed-sleeping porch and oodles of charm. I had saved twenty percent for the down payment. But I wanted to put even more down.

My parents drove up to look at the house. My father refused to go inside.

"In a city filled with brick homes, you chose wood shingles? The maintenance and money this home will require is ridiculous. You're not ready to own a home."

He got back in the car.

I was hurt and upset, but I was also ready to trust my gut because I'd learned from the best in the business.

My father may have known how to invest, but he didn't understand the intangibles, I realized. His way of life and cost of living were stuck in a time warp. The family house he'd built in a fading town had actually lost money. Real estate I knew better than him, and I ended up tripling my money when I sold it.

I sent my dad a report on the home's value five years after I bought it. He was impressed, though he never said so. I knew because he bought me a subscription to *Value Line*, an investment newsletter. I read it every day, like the sports section. I maxed out my retirement option at work. I saved an extra ten percent above that. But, like a lifetime minor-league player who was constantly scrapping, there wasn't a lot of fun playing in my dad's farm system. I didn't travel. I didn't buy a thing. I became obsessed with saving. I studied companies as closely as a gambler might study horses at the track: I knew everything about Boeing, Johnson & Johnson and Coca-Cola. I bought early stocks in Walmart, J.B. Hunt, Starbucks.

I rarely went out with my friends. I saw dollars attached to everything. Why would I pay four bucks for a beer when I could buy a six-pack for the same price?

I met one of my best friends from college for happy hour in St. Louis one fall day when I was considering switching jobs. I had a goal: increase my salary by twenty percent every two to three years with a job change. I had a good offer.

"Dude, your obsession with money is getting weird. Unhealthy. Like, bat-shit crazy unhealthy," he said, in only the way he could. "How much do you need to be happy?"

"It could all go away tomorrow," I said.

"No, you could *die* tomorrow," he said. "And everything

you saved and planned for wouldn't mean a thing, because you never really lived."

That should've changed me profoundly. Instead, I thought, *What if I live to ninety? I'll need a lot of money to live well until then.*

Ironically, the only frivolous thing I ever spent money on, and on which my father approved, was sports. I bought season tickets to the Cardinals and the Blues, and when the Rams came to St. Louis, I spent an insane amount of money to ante up for a PSL—personal seat license—to give me the option to purchase tickets. My father always sent me his pref list of games to attend.

One of my best friends once asked my father, "Are you coming to St. Louis to see your son or the Cardinals?"

It was one of those simple questions that hit like a laser. My father didn't answer.

To fill that gnawing need for attention and respect, I did change jobs every few years. I not only wanted to make more money and take on more responsibility, I wanted the validation of feeling worthy.

My father was of the era that you stayed with a company for life, and so my constant movement was jarring to him. But he liked that my income was steadily increasing. In my thirties, I was earning more money than he was, I had a better retirement plan than he did and I had better medical than he did.

When we'd watch ballgames together, we'd often spread our portfolios before us and analyze them, much like a manager might his lineup. We may have approached our careers differently, but we had common ground.

And then I came out, met my husband, Gary, and wrote and sold my first book.

This was too much for my father. The embarrassing public shame of my sexuality may have been one thing, but my looming career and financial decision was just as monstrous in his eyes.

My father always knew I wanted to write, but he thought I had placed it in the back of my head, like how a kid abandons their toys when they get a bit too old.

"It's like you're spitting in my face," my father told me when I announced my plan to write full-time.

"Because I want to be happy? Live my dream?"

"Because you'll lose everything."

And that's when I finally understood: fear ruled my father's life. He didn't change jobs because he loved his so much. He was scared to do it. He didn't move because he was scared. He didn't travel because he was scared. The one thing he could control was his money.

No, strike that. The only thing he believed he could control me with was his money.

"You're out of my trust," my father then told me.

I knew it was a real threat because he smiled when he said it. I half believed he was even going to pump his fist as if he'd just struck out a batter in the bottom of the ninth with the tying run at third.

October 2015

The Cardinals are in trouble in the bottom of the second. They're up 2-1 now, but the Cubs have two men on and Javier Baez up to bat. The Wrigley faithful are roaring.

"Turn the damn game off. I'd rather not witness this train wreck live."

I've heard the same thing my whole life.

"Game's over," he says. "Cubs lineup is filled with superstars. Team threw money at them. Everyone hates showoffs and grandstanders."

I turn my head from the game, the Wrigley fans going bonkers, and look at my father, whose face is solemn, as if he's a preacher putting on a show at church. He is staring directly at me.

I can read his expression.

What kind of real man writes for a living?

He could never understand what I did for a living. He could never understand how I made a living. Before we moved from St. Louis, before we were to find out my mom was sick with cancer, I took my parents to a Cards game in

2005. The team was very good that year. They would go on to win one hundred games, Albert Pujols would win the MVP, Chris Carpenter the Cy Young. When he was happily drunk, I told him that my husband, Gary, and I would be leaving St. Louis and moving to Michigan. I was quitting my job. I was becoming a full-time writer.

He got so drunk, vendors stopped serving him.

The next day, as I lay in bed in our tiny bungalow, I heard Gary—the only person to wake before my father—make coffee. My dad, even with a hangover, rose at dawn. I could hear the two murmur. I got out of bed and stuck my head to the crack of the door.

"Aren't you proud of your son?" Gary asked, in only the way he could, kind, gentle, searching for peace and understanding.

"No," my father said bluntly.

"Why?"

"He should work nine to five," my father said. "A real man works a real job."

"Do you know how hard your son works? How hard he has worked to make his dream come true? He works from four in the morning until midnight."

"Not the way a real man does it."

"Why?" Gary asked.

"That's the way it is done," my dad said.

"No, that's the way it *was* done," Gary replied.

"No, that's the way it should be done," my dad said, his voice rising.

There was silence.

"You worked for an entrepreneur, didn't you?" Gary asked.

Silence.

"And what was it like for him in the beginning? What do you think he heard from his friends and family? Don't do it. You'll fail. It'll never work. You'll lose everything. And how did it turn out?"

"That's different," my father yelled. "He was an engineer, a man of science. He started a business."

"That's what your son is doing," Gary said. "Do you know that by landing an agent and selling a book to a major publisher your son has already accomplished what 99.9 percent of writers fail to achieve?" He stopped. "Who supported your boss in the beginning?"

"His wife," my father said.

"And I'm Wade's husband. And I will tell you this— your son would walk through walls to make this succeed and to take care of me. Your son will not fail because he doesn't know how to fail. And do you know where he learned that? You!"

Silence.

"Say you're proud of your son," Gary said.

Silence.

"Say you're proud of your son!" Gary yelled. Long silence. "Okay, Ted. Then I will say it every single day for the rest of his life until Wade not only hears it but also starts to believe it."

My mother was so unnerved by my father's reaction to my life, Gary and my career, that she changed her trust on her deathbed. My father still got everything, but she made it clear that, after his death, the money she had saved and invested would go directly to me. He would not have the final say.

Why, I wondered, *didn't my mother trust him? He knew money. He may have been angry, but he would always do what was right. Right?*

One night just days before she died, my mother motioned for me to come close, then closer. She mustered her energy to grab my forearm, tight.

"Wade, hear this—death brings out the worst in those who are left behind," she told me, her voice hoarse, wheezing for air. "But money always reveals the truth."

My father was incensed. He felt we had collaborated behind his back. We had turned on him. Wife and son. It was *Game of Thrones* to him. But my mother was dying, and she was my only concern.

Gary and I set up cots in my mother's room at an assisted living facility she had picked to die in. In the midst of the horror, my mom would wake up the last month of her life around midnight, lucid and alert, ready to talk. We would order milkshakes, and she would tell us stories about her life, about my brother and me as babies. Often, she would shoo Gary out of the room, and she would tell me that God had planned for it to come down to me and my father. She made it sound like the future of the world, good versus evil, was at stake.

"It's not Star Wars," I would joke. "Luke and Darth Vader."

"No, it's bigger," she would say, "because it's real. Father and son. You always do the right thing. Your father tries, but it doesn't come easily. Will he do the right thing in the end? Will he do the right thing by you? I hope so, I pray he will, but I don't know, so I want you to be prepared," she told me, as clear as a bell. "I want you to know you will likely have every right—and every opportunity—to walk away from your father after I'm gone, and no one, not even me or God, would blame you. But I think you might be the only one able to save him. If you're up to it."

"You're scaring me," I told her.

"Good," she said.

Mostly, however, she would tell me how proud she was of me those last weeks of her life, words I craved, soaked up, like lupine in the desert. I had just published my third memoir, a humorous look at moving from the city to the woods of Michigan to be a sort of modern-day Thoreau. The book was doing well, both critically and sales-wise, but we had put our tour on hold. On one of the final Saturdays of my mother's life, we gathered in her room to watch the weekend *Today* show. My memoir had been selected as a summer read by the NBC program. My mother wept. Her friends applauded. My father didn't show.

My mother, naturally, had planned her own funeral. Ever the good mom and hospice nurse, she didn't want to add more stress to our pain. I executed every detail.

Like every good Ozarks funeral, my mother had an open casket. In the Ozarks, we like to say that the funeral homes can "lay out a good body." At the end of the funeral, after everyone had wept, hugged and paid their respects, I walked up to my mother, kissed her on the cheek and pulled a button off her dress.

Before Gary and I left, my father made a pot of weak coffee and then he rather reluctantly walked us to our car. I opened my arms to hug him, and he took a step back.

"Just know we may not talk for a while," he said.

He was so hurt, so lost, so alone and so angry. I was, too.

"I never wanted your money, Dad. If I'm out of your trust forever, so be it. And I would never ask Mom to do anything to hurt you." I looked at him. "I just want you to know how much I loved her. I want you to know how much I love you."

"You two..." he started, before shaking his head and stopping, leaving me to wonder whether the completion of his statement would have been a positive one or not.

"Now it's the two of us, Dad," I said, finishing for him. "I loved Mom more than anything in this world, but I still have you. And you still have me. And, believe it or not, you taught me to be a survivor. I need you to be strong now not only for yourself but also for me and Mom."

He nodded, turned and walked back inside the house.

A few weeks later, I walked to our country mailbox in Michigan, a hike from our cottage in the woods. When I opened the box, I found two pieces of mail. One was no-tification of a change in my father's trust, letting me know I had been removed as a successor. The other was the button from my mother's dress that I had left at my father's house when I was grief-stricken.

No two pieces of mail could have summed up my complicated father more. He loved me, but he was also teaching me a lesson. He was still in charge of his finances. But in sending me that simple button, he was also expressing his love for me in the only way he knew how, like when he bought me those cars.

I thought of my mother and grandmother as I sank to the ground holding those two pieces of mail, a document that to me still seemed as unreal as a pot of gold at the end of a rainbow, as well as a button that was more valuable to me than any money in the world. I leaned against the wood post holding up our country mailbox, their voices echoing in my head.

"Look at this beautiful button, Wade," my grandma was saying. *"All forgotten. All with a story. All from someone and somewhere. These hold value, these things that just get tossed aside. Never forget that."*

And:

"Wade, hear this—death brings out the worst in those who are left behind, but money always reveals the truth. I want you to know you will likely have every right—and every opportunity—to walk away from your father after I'm gone, and no one, not even me or God, would blame you. But I think you might be the only one able to save him."

3RD INNING

"When the Going Gets Tough..."

October 2015

In the blink of an eye, Javier Baez hits a three-run homer, and the Cubs are suddenly up 4-2. The irony is rich. Baez is a product of the Cubs farm system. They drafted him. They developed him. And now he was turning on the Cardinals *and* my father.

The Cubs fans are roaring into the top of the third.

"Turn off the damn game!" my father yells. "I can't take another minute of it!"

I don't.

In the past, he would have been in control of the television. He would've muted the game, thrown the remote or, most likely, turned it off and walked away.

This is my father's MO.

While my defense mechanism may have been humor, my father's coping mechanism was avoidance. If he ignored it, it wasn't real. But it was: as an empath, it was as if I were holding a microscope up to my father's soul, and I could see that all the hurt, pain and tumult were real even if he pretended they weren't.

Despite all of his tough talk and outward bravado, my father was deeply wounded. But when the going got tough, he had no way to express it. So he drank to block out the pain. It was easier to click off the TV, and life, than confront his emotions head-on.

It was learned behavior in the Ozarks.

Growing up, my grampa had a few bluetick hounds he used for hunting. Most blueticks are relentless hunters, and particularly fearless, pursuing anything larger and fiercer than them, even bears. They are also excellent night hunters, with extremely good eyesight. But one of my grampa's blueticks was an aberration: it was scared of anything that stood up to it, and it would hightail it and run at the slightest sound, the crack of a branch or the crunch of some leaves. It also developed cataracts at an early age. My grandma took the dog inside, and at night, it would sit at the window and bay at the moon, a soulful, haunting call that could stretch for minutes at a time.

"Dog ain't got no damn sense," my grampa would say, shaking his head. "All bark and no bite."

When he would walk away, my grandma would always say, "Stop!" and the dog would stop. Then she would sneak that dog a cookie and say, "Maybe it has all the dang sense in the world. It knows when it's beat, and its barkin' got it exactly what it wanted—a place inside the house. No questions asked. Just knows how to work a crowd."

My dad had a lot in common with that bluetick hound, but I felt—like my grandma—I was the only who could see it or deal with it in the right way.

"Turn the damn game off!" he yells again.

Whenever the Cards got behind in a game, he got a beer. Whenever they fell too far behind, he simply clicked off the radio or TV and tuned out the bad stuff.

I remember the night the Cardinals were in a slugfest with the Philadelphia Phillies. The entire Rouse family had gathered at our cabin on Sugar Creek to celebrate the Fourth of July. Aunts, uncles and cousins from Indianapolis and Austin had traveled back home to fish, make homemade ice cream, canoe and shoot fireworks. The game was blaring, we were all laughing, and the echo of bottle rockets off the bluffs filled the air. My brother never made it. After ending his shift at his summer job, he was hit while driving his motorcycle on a one-lane bridge by a sleepy truck driver. Life over before it had even begun at the age of seventeen.

At first, I thought the flashing police lights were fireworks.

My father refused to talk about it. Acknowledge it. Grieve for too long. My mother couldn't get out of bed for weeks, but my father returned to work almost immediately. I now understand that there are many different ways to cope with grief, but I also now understand that my father never dealt with his at all. My father never discussed Todd, as if he had not been born.

My brother was bigger than life to me as a kid. He was my protector. And yet he taught me how to fight. He was a country boy. And yet he taught me to love nature and expressed such deep love for me. We had a historic snowfall one winter, the depth nearly reaching my tiny chest.

I was both mesmerized and terrified. My brother carried me into the middle of the yard and plopped me into the snow, retrieved a stepladder and helped me make a snowman that was the envy of the town.

"I got the muscle," he said, "but you got the magic. Tell me how it should look."

"Like us," I said. "I want it to look like the two of us."

My father never seemed to remember such moments.

"How many children do you have?" a stranger might ask us at the Piggly-Wiggly after the accident.

"One," my dad would always quickly answer. "Just the one."

Just the one.

I did the same. For years, close friends in college believed I was an only child.

It wasn't a lie, I convinced myself. It was simply hitting Mute on the remote or changing the channel.

To cope with my brother's loss, along with my burgeoning sexuality, I ate. A lot. Much more than I had as a chubby kid. I gained weight at an alarming rate. I did it to fill the giant hole of pain and anger that would not go away, but I also ate to disappear. If my father could blunt his pain with booze and complete avoidance, I could blunt mine with Pringles, French-onion dip, Little Debbies, ice cream and Count Chocula.

But I also ate to make myself invisible. My brother was everything I was not: A man's man. A hunter. A fisherman. My brother was going to give my parents everything I knew I never could: A wife, grandchildren, a legacy. So

I also ate to lessen the anguish I knew I would one day bring to my parents.

Mostly, I blamed God for not taking me. I was the bad kid, after all, the gay one, the one destined for hell, the one my father did not like. *Why Todd? Why not me?*

But all of that was not discussed either. Life had to maintain its routine. My father didn't have time for tragedy.

He did have time for the Cardinals, however. In the weeks after my brother's death, while my mother remained in bed unable to cope with her grief, her wrist heavily bandaged from where she had shattered a vase and tried to slash it with a jagged piece, my dad began to ask out loud if we should go to St. Louis for a game.

He dearly loved the 1979 Cardinals team. It was filled with talent but highly inconsistent, winning in waves and then losing in stretches.

That year's team was filled with Cardinals icons: Ted "Simba" Simmons, Keith Hernandez, Lou Brock, Garry Templeton, Ken Oberkfell, George Hendrick, Bob Forsch.

The longer my mother remained in bed, the more agitated my father became.

I returned home a few weeks after Todd died after spending a weekend with my grandparents in Sugar Creek to find my brother was quite literally gone from our home. All the photos of him had been removed. Only ghostly silhouettes remained on the wall. His closet had been emptied. I found his beloved guitar hidden in the corner of our attic. I moved it to my room, and when I opened the windows, the breeze made the strings strum.

I could hear my brother speak to me.

I didn't want his voice silenced, or his memory erased. I needed him with me.

And then one evening after returning home from work, my dad tossed some of his clothes into a garbage bag and asked me to do the same.

"Where are we going?" I asked.

"Cardinals game," he said.

"No!"

"You're gettin' in the damn car," he said.

I had no choice.

I wept the entire trip to St. Louis for leaving my mother in bed, for abandoning her, for not fighting harder to keep my brother alive in our home.

My father drove, not saying a word, until we reached a motel on the outskirts of the city.

The first game we attended was an afternoon game. My father bought nosebleed seats near the top of the old Busch Stadium. The city was always magical to me as a kid. My town consisted of a few-block stretch of Main Street and a flashing light. St. Louis stretched out for infinity. The Arch and the towering buildings resembled things I only saw in the movies. People were diverse and dressed in high fashion. There were restaurants offering food of every variety. My father got lost on the interstate every single time. He cursed the magnitude of the city. It called to me.

I wore vests and birdwing-collared shirts that my grandmothers made for me. My dad wore stained T-shirts and sunglasses held together by safety pins.

"Look at these freaks," my dad would say as we walked around the city, people staring at us.

I loved the old Busch Stadium. Ninety-six arches, the "Crown of Arches," ringed the roof, echoing the Gateway Arch, which rose from beyond the outfield—shimmering in the sunlight—like a curved path to heaven. As the sun moved in the sky, the shadow of the roof was tossed onto the Astroturf, and mini arches shadowed the playing field.

These presented a nightmare for the players. Batters had to stare out at a pitcher's mound in blaring light and hit a ball as it traveled into the shadows. Outfielders had to track a ball that went from sun to shade in an instant.

The day we attended was one of those oppressively humid St. Louis afternoons. The stadium felt like a rain forest.

My father wore an old Cards cap—once bright red that had faded to pink—with the STL logo atop his head. My father never wore his cap correctly. He didn't tug it down over his head or break its bill. He simply placed it atop his head, as one might lay a dish on a dining table.

I sported my beloved Brockabrella, a sun umbrella popularized by Lou Brock that I had purchased years earlier. It was part umbrella, part hat that towered over your head like a pop-up tent. It protected you from the sun and rain.

And it came in a deluge that afternoon. Thunderstorms broke out. A rain delay was called. Water slid off my Brockabrella as I watched players slide around the field. My father didn't mind. It gave him more time to drink beer.

But then I noticed it, what at first I thought were raindrops cascading down my father's face. He was crying. The first time I had seen him do so in public. I finally realized that my dad had asked me to run away to a ballgame with him so his wife and no one in our small town could see him mourn the loss of his eldest son. The sky was weeping, and so was my father. He didn't want to see a game. He wanted to be with me in order to share a moment that might give him a sliver of hope, a reason to live.

As the rain slowed, my father held out the beer to me. "Don't tell your mother."

Summer 1970

I would guess I was around the age of five when my father pulled me from swim lessons.

When I say my father pulled me from swim lessons, I mean that literally: he showed up one Friday midmorning in his suit and pulled me from the pool.

"This boy don't need fancy," he said.

My mother had enrolled me at a "fancy place" in the biggest city closest to our rural town of about a thousand people. It was a sort of a country club, with a pool, swimming lessons, tennis courts, an adjoining golf course and a place for folks to lunch.

Ironically, my father was quite an accomplished golfer who played with his company in tournaments across the Midwest. But he preferred to play at a nearby no-frills nine-hole course.

My mother wanted me to learn to swim since our family's summers were largely spent at my grandparents' cabin, not much more than a spit away from a fast-moving, ice-cold creek.

"Too dangerous for unwatched kids," she would always say.

My mother also welcomed the tiny break swim lessons provided her. She was raising us children, working as a nurse and spending most every weekend with her parents or my father's parents. Looking back, she was still a young woman who needed friends her own age. I needed friends my own age.

"Your mom don't need fancy friends either," he told me. "You will not end up bein' spoiled."

So he pulled me dripping from that pool—as my mom and our new friends looked on—loaded me up and took me to his office for the rest of the day before packing me into the old Rambler to take me to the creek.

He didn't even take me inside the cabin. He grabbed the six-pack he had purchased at a liquor store on the way down, pulled the tab off one, stuck one in each trouser pocket and dropped the remaining three in the icy freshwater spring where we kept our minnows, milk and soda.

"I learned to swim on my own!" he said. "You'll do the damn same. Kids today are too spoiled. You don't need coddling. You need ice water in your veins."

He grabbed my hand and led me across the rocky beach that separated the creek from the bluff on which our cabin was perched. The beach was filled with polished stones and arrowheads. It was where we gathered to lay out, light bonfires, set off fireworks, clean fish, launch a canoe or jump on inner tubes.

"Feet 'a clay!" he exclaimed as we marched. "You could walk on fire."

I may have been a "soft" kid, but my dad loved that I could march across those rocks without a wince or an "ouch" as if I were marching on the softest sand beach in the Hamptons. When I attempted to play football, I broke my finger so badly the bones protruded through the skin. I may have been sensitive, but I was not weak. The coach called my dad first. He was at work.

"Still attached to your body, right, boy?" he asked. "You're tough, ain't ya?"

"Yes," I said.

"You can play through the pain," he said.

My mom showed up twenty minutes later and screamed at the coach for not calling 911. I had to have surgery—complete with staples—to rebuild a finger.

But I learned as I grew older it was better not to cry. If you could act tough, you could be tough.

Sugar Creek—or "crick" as my dad called it—was, in high water, a wide, fast-moving ribbon, more akin to a river. On the other side of the crick was acres of pastoral land filled with tall grasses, Queen Anne's lace and wildflowers that swayed in the wind. This summer had been, like most Ozarks summers, muggy, and filled with thunderstorms. Every day felt like a warm washcloth.

When we reached the creek, my father set down his beer, picked me up without warning and tossed me in.

I remember popping my eyes open, panicked. Below me were the pretty, polished stones I loved to collect with my mom when the water was low.

All of a sudden, water filled my nostrils and mouth. I popped to the surface, choking.

"Help me!" I yelled at my dad, the fast current carrying me downstream.

He was seated on the edge of the bank, leaned back, relaxed, drinking his beer, as if he were watching the sunset.

"Help me, Daddy!" I continued to yell.

"Swim, boy!" he said, disgusted. "Hard!"

He made no move to assist me. I didn't even see him flinch.

I was never scared of the water. I had spent my childhood on inner tubes and in canoes, fishing, jumping off rocks into my mother's waiting arms.

But Sugar Creek was a swift current, especially in front of our cabin, and it didn't slow until it slinked around a rocky bend where the water got deep and dark. I had never swum in water that deep. My brother used to tell me that it went straight to the center of the earth, and there was a whirlpool in the middle that would suck you down.

I began to swim.

I swam against that current, as hard as I could, until my shoulders ached and my lungs burned, and I didn't stop churning until my little belly was scraping the bottom. When I finally looked up, I had reached the far edge of our beach, where a little finger of rocks reached out into the water as if to save me. It was shallow enough to stand.

I walked over to my father, who had yet to move a muscle, and collapsed on the beach beside him. I lay back and—even though I knew better—sobbed.

He started to laugh harder than I'd ever heard him laugh.

"Now that was a damn sight," he said. "Stop your caterwaulin', boy."

He finished his beer and then popped another one. When I stopped crying, he looked at me and said, "Ya didn't die, did ya?"

He held out his beer.

"Take it, boy," he said. "You earned it."

I took a sip.

"Don't tell your mother," he said.

I knew he wasn't talking about the beer.

Summer 2010

Forty years later, I was in northern Michigan. It was a very warm late-September day. I had gone swimming in much-too-wavy waters in Lake Michigan. There were red flag warnings. Gary was angry at my lack of caution. He refused to talk to me when I emerged, uttering only, "Are you crazy? You could have died!" before rolling away from me on his beach towel.

Later, we had strolled Fishtown in Leland, a charming resort town in northern Michigan filled with historic fishing shanties. The salmon were running. They raced upstream from the lake and were trying to jump over a dam to reach the river. They kept jumping, over and over and over, flailing. And then they would try again, pummeling themselves, hoping against hope, dying to make the impossible happen.

"What's going on?" Gary asked.

"That's me," I said. "Those fish are me."

He looked at me, not understanding. I had never told him my story.

What they were doing, I realized, was pure instinct. They would die because they had to reach a place that was engrained inside of them.

I understood.

Don't ever give up.

Fight.

Survive.

Just go against the current and try to surface.

Don't cry.

You've got to do it on your own.

I thought that was just how everyone lived.

But it was then I finally understood: I never really learned how to swim.

I just learned how not to drown.

October 2015

It's time for my father's nightly meds. The caretaker has them neatly arranged in a pill box, organized by day of the week. This isn't your ordinary pill box. It's gigantic, the pill box equivalent of an old Lincoln Continental.

My father takes a boatload of pills every few hours. He takes pills for his blood pressure and his cholesterol, pills to make his blood clot and pills to soften his stool, pills for his dementia and pills to stimulate his appetite.

Growing up, my father refused to take even a children's vitamin. My mother would place a Flintstone chewable out on the plastic cutting board next to a coffee mug ringed with little white daisies, a butter knife and an English muffin in hopes that he would at least ingest something somewhat healthy into his body.

There were many weekend mornings when I would wake, and my father would be sipping both a coffee and a beer.

Stimulant and depressant going at the same time. If there was a chorus to my father's life song, that would be it: *Stim-*

*ulant and depressant, high and low, open my mouth and watch
me go.*

My father has abused alcohol most of his life, but it went
unchecked and unchallenged because he simply changed
the channel when it was discussed. We ignored the issue
directly in front of our faces like we did any problem in
our lives: his drinking, my weight, my mother's smoking.
We ran a shell game to con each other, thinking each of
us were winning when, in reality, we were all losers. As
a sober person, Gary made me deal with my demons. He
helped me respect myself and lose 120 pounds. He helped
me make amends. He talked to my father after one New
Year's Eve debacle when Dad made a scene in a restaurant
and then woke up with severe tremors only to pour another Bloody Mary.

"Only family talks to family, boy," my dad told Gary.
"And you ain't family."

Over the years, the weekend six-pack at the cabin turned
into a nightly six-pack. Then beer turned to vodka, and
vodka to whiskey, and then they were all just mixed together and poured directly into his tiny midcentury shaker
of a body.

In his later years, pills were added. Ativan was prescribed
for my father's anxiety, a diagnosis that always made me
shake my head. His whole life, my dad was as high-strung
as a Chihuahua in a thunderstorm, which was why he
drank. After my mother died, he went from doctor to doctor, telling them he couldn't sleep, gathering Ativan like a
squirrel does nuts for the winter, hiding them all over the
house. Those were washed down by his drink of choice.

Until…

I pull all of his evening meds together and bring them to him in a tiny little desert rose dish that used to be his mother's. He eyes me warily—as he does every single care-taker—as if we are planning to poison him.

I would've already done it, old man. And an entire bullpen of people would have helped me.

He sticks out his tongue, and I put a pill on the end.

He swallows it dry, forgetting there is water coming. I pat him on the back, over and over. He hacks and hacks, so loud and so long, Gary has to come out to check.

"I got it," I say. "Go back to your room." I look at Gary. "I'd hate to interrupt your texting."

Gary smiles and mouths, "You okay?"

I shake my head no; he laughs and disappears.

I hold up a big water bottle with a flexible straw to my father's mouth. He takes a tiny sip.

"One more."

He shoots me the Rouse death glance and takes an even smaller sip.

I shake my head.

I've never seen my father drink a whole glass of water in his entire life. This is no exaggeration. Despite growing up around creeks, streams, rivers and lakes, my father acts as if water is poisonous. For years, he would glare at me when I would walk in carrying a water bottle, a look of confusion on his face when I'd grab a La Croix over a Bud.

"Why have you always hated water?" I ask him.

"Tasteless," he says.

The word seems meant for me.

"The man is like a kangaroo rat," my mother used to say.

My mom had an Ozarks way—which I term as combining the gentility of the South with the directness of southwest Missouri—of going to the heart of the matter in a nonoffensive way. She was the queen of insignificant trivia—such as the state flower of Idaho, the fiber content of brussels sprouts or the fact a kangaroo rat can survive without any water—and her delivery of bizarre, off-the-cuff remarks was cutting, funny and oh-so-true.

My mother loved calling my father an "old goat-witch," believing he was not born but rather created over a cauldron by a group of witches who wanted to make the most stubborn and mischievous creature possible.

I hold the water up for my father, and he takes another baby sip.

Jason Heyward walks for the Cards in the top of the third. My father's eyes widen as he takes his pills. Heyward is immediately picked off first base to end the inning.

"Turn it off!" my father yells, before choking again.

I hold up the water bottle.

My mother cared for my father for decades. As a nurse, it was in her DNA. She nurtured people. She believed Ozarks folk had lived harder lives than most. They had not enjoyed opportunities others took for granted. Food on the table, running water, a roof without holes, those were the good life for many, my mom believed. As a nurse, she was often on-call, meaning she would have to go into work on holidays or weekends if there was an accident and she was needed. But she was always on-call generally. Townsfolk rang her when they lopped off a finger with a chainsaw or shot themselves in the leg while hunting. She would race out of the house, cooler in hand, to retrieve and ice the digit. My mom was the primary caretaker for all of my grandparents. She was the one who would jump in the car to help my grampa, a hypochondriac if there ever was one, to assure him he wasn't having a heart attack and ease him back to sleep at two in the morning.

But my father struggled to spend a day with her as she lay dying.

He was a creature of habit, and when his routine was disturbed—even by the death of his wife—he simply couldn't deal, like so many men of his era with their emotions. Coping meant numbing. Dealing meant running. He had to get the paper, retrieve the mail, mow the lawn, pay the bills, do all the things he normally did as if it were just another typical Tuesday.

I filled my mom's days with her favorite things: friends, ice cream, coffee and conversation. When she could no longer walk, Gary and I pampered her with treatments—hair, manicure, pedicure, massage, facial—that she would never do for herself because it didn't adhere to my father's budget.

My devotion was often met with mistrust and skepticism.

"Go home, boy," he would say to me after Gary and I had spent a week sleeping on cots the assisted living facility had set up for us in a spare room.

"I am home," I would say.

I feed the pills to my father, slowly. He's like a baby with a bottle. I feed, he drinks, he spits, I wipe, he continues. Rinse and repeat.

It is a slow process. When Cards pitcher John Lackey walks the leadoff hitter in the bottom of the third, I finally finish giving him his pills. He tilts his head like a child, his signal to me that he doesn't want any more water. My father still looks like a little boy sometimes. The soft curl of his light hair. His blue eyes. That mischievous look. There is a photo I have of him when he was little eating an ice cream cone as big as his head. He is standing in the middle of the street, shirtless and wearing overalls, tongue out covered with ice cream, dimpled and smiling from ear to ear. When I look at my dad right now, he doesn't look that much different.

He keeps his head tilted away from me and the TV.

"I told you to turn it off, boy."

"Want some ice cream?" I ask.

He scooches his head just an inch or so toward me. "Yeah!"

I bring him a bowl and start to feed him.

Sometimes, this closeness with my father still makes me uncomfortable. The intimacy seems rippled with tension. It feels all too little, too late. Sometimes, I still want to shove this entire bowl of ice cream down my throat to numb my pain, fill the void, gag the words that have always been too hard to say.

My father eats but refuses to look at the TV.

Or me. I'm too close for comfort.

When I came out, my father refused to talk to me for over two years.

"You have shamed the family," he said.

My mother ended up running away from home because

she could not stand making undercover calls from work. I could not stand taking them.

So she got on a Greyhound bus, came to St. Louis, met and fell in love—like I did—with Gary.

"He's making me choose," she told me. "It's him or you."

"What are you going to do?" I asked her.

"I'm here, aren't I?" she said.

We've already forgotten that was the way it was for many families. Dads were disgusted. Moms had to choose: Marriage or divorce. Husband or child. A way of life they knew or a new life they'd never known.

It was a choice no one should ever be asked to make. Because it isn't a choice. It's your child.

My mother stayed a week and, before she left, said, "I feel as if I finally got to see my son for the first time in my life." After she returned home, my father wrote me a chilling letter. He told me I would forever live my life in darkness. He wrote I would never be at peace. He said I would lose my job and all of my friends. He said, before I burned in hell, I must live the rest of my life without his approval, his love or his money. He told me he would never see me or speak to me again.

"Choose wisely," he said.

But, really, I had never chosen.

I was always who I was. The only choice he left me with was to live with the man I loved or without the family I loved.

Like my mom, I had already made my choice.

But that was why I have succeeded in a career where others have failed. You lose a brother, you nearly lose a family, and the big challenges in life don't seem so big any longer. The rejection of a book or a magazine essay is tiny compared to the loss of your family and the foundation upon which you were raised.

But over time, I began to understand that my father never had a choice either. He was raised in a time and place in which being gay was not even real. What tools did he have to cope with me? What friends did he have to talk to about it? What common experiences did he have to help shape his understanding?

None.

My friends who had been out and proud long before there were even terms for that would get angry when I would defend my father. But how does a person who's never picked up a bat in his life be expected to stand at the plate and hit a fastball from Nolan Ryan?

My family were Ozarks through and through, meaning their perspective and experiences were pinned to the land. The world around them looked and talked and thought just like they did.

My experiences since I had left home—college, graduate school in Chicago, living in St. Louis—had changed me greatly. My mirror reflected a different person and world.

So I always gave my father a little more rope, wondering if he would climb to a new understanding.

I always gave him one more chance.

Lackey gets the Cubs' Kris Bryant to hit into a double play. He then strikes out Anthony Rizzo to end the third.

"That's why I didn't turn off the TV," I say, pumping my fist into the air. "There's always a chance."

My father shakes his head at me.

"Right?" I ask. "What do you think?"

His dimples grow.

I hold my breath.

He's going to say something that will make it all right, make all this hurt disappear. He's not going to walk away from his emotions for once. He's going to confront them, be transparent with me. He's going to hit a walk-off homer in the bottom of the ninth to win the game. He is finally grabbing the rope I've left dangling for decades.

"More?" he asks, nodding at his bowl of ice cream.

I think of the photo of him as a kid.

Maybe people don't change. Maybe I've been played for a fool my whole life. Maybe ignoring everything you feel is the only way to survive this long.

In the distance, I can hear a hound bay.

"Sure thing, Dad," I say.

4TH INNING

"Team History"

October 2015

"How many games they played, boy? Cards 'n Cubs? Venture a guess?"

My dad is more alert after ice cream and meds.

"A couple thousand?"

He shakes his head at me.

"I'm asking you. You should know your damn history."

I grab my cell and look it up. And wait. My father doesn't have internet service. Gary and I finally secured the password to a neighbor's.

"I was right," I say. "Well over two thousand. First meeting was in Sportsman's Park in 1892. Says the economic trade rivalry between the cities of Chicago and St. Louis led to the formation of the St. Louis Brown Stockings and the Chicago White Stockings. Wanna know when their first postseason matchup was?"

My dad nods.

"This is it," I say. "Only took about 120 years."

"I'll be damned," my dad says. "Lived to see it."

I laugh. "They waited long enough, didn't they, Dad?" I stop. "Waited for you."

My dad shakes his head and tugs at the bill. "How many pennants they win?"

I look at my cell and read to him. "The Cardinals are the oldest major league team west of the Mississippi River. They've won 11 World Series titles and 23 pennants, second only to the New York Yankees."

"You should know that off the top a' yer head, boy," my dad says. "You should know your damn history. Haven't I taught you anything?"

You should know your damn history.

This was one of my father's mantras. He would often quiz me, like he would with the periodic table, on the same subjects: Ozarks history, sports history, family history.

At least one Saturday a month, fall through winter, after we'd closed the cabin down for summer and school was in session, my father would load the family into the car after a big, hot breakfast. He despised oatmeal as much as powdered milk, things he subsisted on growing up when there wasn't much money. He loved his weekend breakfasts: dollar-sized pancakes with hot blueberry sauce, bacon and eggs, Belgian waffles with ham. As he ate, my father would scribble in pencil on a napkin. The end result resembled something that a hamster might have drawn if you handed it the same pencil, but it made total sense to my father. It was a map. Of his childhood.

My dad would load me and my brother into the old Rambler and ramble off into the Ozarks countryside, napkin stuffed in the cigarette tray. We would drive through the neighborhoods where he grew up, alongside creeks where he had fished and floated.

"Caught my big bass right there!" he'd yell, pointing at a deep, still part of the water in the middle of nowhere.

"Got caught in the drain over there playing as a kid!" he'd yell, pointing at a storm sewer. "Had to call the police to get me loose."

"Used to sled down that hill after a big snow!" he'd yell. "Broke three fingers!"

Many Saturdays, though, my dad would drive until the paved roads became dirt and the dirt roads became chat and the chat roads became fields and the fields became creek beds with a few inches of running water.

"Don't worry," he'd say, as we bumped along, the ride so rocky I'd hit my head on the top of the Rambler. "I know where I'm going."

Usually, there were stories attached to the places we went to.

"I used to come here and quail hunt with your grampa," or "I kissed a girl right there under that weepin' willow." Or he'd tell us how a collapsing motel on a bluff that could now be rented for a buck a night used to be a resort where famous country singers came for the prime rib and fried fish.

But many times, my dad would just stop the car and stare out the window.

He saw things no longer apparent to us. Ghosts to me. History to him.

He was the same with family.

Ozarks men rarely shared more than a beer with another, but my father would make me sit by my grandfathers on their birthdays and on Father's Day. He'd look at them every single year and say, "Tell 'im. Tell the boy 'bout what you went through."

And they would go through the histories of their lives.

My grandparents were working poor. My grampa Shipman was an ore miner in the little town where I grew up, and when that dried up, he raked rocks from farmers' land and then hand tilled the soil. It was backbreaking work. In fact, the hands of he and my grandma were thick as grapevines, their fingers knotted like sassafras.

My grampa Shipman was a country man through and through. He smoked unfiltered cigarettes, drank whiskey like it was water and cursed a blue streak. He was rough. Not actor-in-a-country-movie-acting-tough but how-do-I-survive rough.

He castrated his little dog in front of me. Made me watch for some reason as I screamed for help, perhaps to toughen me up, perhaps to show me how tough he was, perhaps because he could get mean when he got drunk.

The dog survived. He named him "Tricky Dick," an ironic nickname for both his fascination with Richard Nixon and what the dog had endured. The dog clung to me whenever I visited.

Sometimes when my dad would make him tell me his stories, my grampa would pull me into his lap and get emotional, a rarity. "It breaks a man not knowin' whether he'll ever see the sunshine again," he would say, his breath thick with whiskey. "You just wanna see the damn light again at the end of the day."

He loved me. Deeply. He just had no way to show that. And when I would cry, he would tell me to look the world in the eye and say, "Fuck you." And when I would whine, he would take me outside and make me rake rocks. "Put your back into it," he'd say.

My grandma Rouse could not escape the memories of the Depression. Even though my grampa worked his way up to become a district manager for the electric company, a job with nice pay and great prestige, my grandma still stole thousands of packets of grape jelly, ketchup, and salt and pepper, stuffing her clutch with every condiment she could get her gloved hands on. She continued to make all of her own clothes, and many of mine, just like she did for her family when they had no money and she would go to the feed store to pick out sacks with the prettiest patterns.

My grampa Rouse taught me to clean fish and skin a squirrel, and how to kill both so they experienced the least amount of pain.

"Square up your shoulders and face it head-on," he would tell me when he'd pull me into his lap, beer in hand, Cards game on the radio. "Face it head-on. Don't you ever turn away from the hard."

When the light would dim and Father's Days would come to a close, my dad would say, "We're done here, boy." Then he'd turn to his father and father-in-law and say, "Thank you, sir, for your time. It's an honor to be part of your family."

September 1998

"He did it! He did it! He did it! He made history!"

I leaped off the couch in the claustrophobic den of our tiny bungalow in St. Louis and raced around the room. I jumped up and down, rattling the old, wavy windows.

"What's going on?" Gary called.

"McGwire did it!" I yelled.

"Who did what?" Gary asked, coming into the TV room. He was holding a spatula thick with cream cheese frosting. Gary may not have appreciated the drama of fall baseball, but he certainly appreciated the drama of a fall dessert.

"McGwire just hit his sixty-second home run! All-time record! Broke Roger Maris's major league record of sixty-one. We may never see this again in our lifetime! And he did it off the Cubs! With Sosa right there to congratulate him."

Gary stared at me. "I understand not a word of what you're saying," he said. He glanced at the TV for a second, the fireworks going off at Busch, the celebration in the stands, the impromptu ceremony, then shook his head. "Men and sports. I'll never understand." He changed his voice to sound like he was narrating an old newsreel from the 1950s. "Sports! Taking the place of real human emotion since the dawn of time. A home run! I can finally hug my father, and act as if it's real!"

I glared at him, and he handed me the spatula. "Sorry," he said. "I'm a little sensitive still. Can you imagine?"

I licked the spatula clean, walked over and hugged him.

We rocked back and forth in front of the TV. It sounded as if the fans were celebrating our love. I spanked Gary with the now-cleaned spatula, and he laughed.

"Pumpkin bars will be ready in a bit," he said.

I took a seat in a little willow rocker and watched my own split screen: Gary baking, and baseball on TV.

Gary, like me, grew up in rural America. He was raised in Southern Illinois, the part of the state that wasn't Chicago or even farmland, it was plumb near Kentucky. His father played sports—baseball, track and college football alongside future Hall of Famers for the Green Bay Packers. He became a teacher and a coach, before earning his doctorate in education and becoming a superintendent. Sports were the backbone of Gary's life growing up. His brother was a good athlete. Gary wanted to draw and paint, but those were verboten for boys in rural America in the 1970s, so he played baseball and got his bones cracked trying to play football.

The first time I visited his parents, Gary showed me photo albums from his youth. There were pages of photos from his "sports days," including a series of old Polaroid photos of him in his first baseball uniform. The photos were taken one after another, almost as if in slow motion, and I joked about how fast his mother's finger must have been working to shoot the old camera that quickly.

But then I saw his face, and my heart shattered. His doe eyes weren't just sad, they were lost and empty. His body was rigid. He was standing like a baseball player should, but it was as though the movements had been taught to a robot. His father was out of the shot, having just thrown

Gary the baseball. It should have been such a happy moment, but there Gary stood, arm outstretched, the ball flying over the top of his glove. Gary's face drooped. His glove dropped. And then he looked off into the neighborhood, as though he wanted to run as far away as he could.

That same night, Gary showed me the calendar he kept his senior year. Huge, red Xs were marked through the days, in deep, disturbing scratches that ripped the paper.

"I counted off every day until I was done living in hell," he said, telling me of all the times he was punched, kicked, spit on, tortured, simply because he was "different," mostly because he stopped playing sports to fit in.

But Gary wasn't done living in hell. He drank. He held retail jobs. He eventually tried to kill himself by putting a razor to his wrist. His mother found him, told him to wear long-sleeved shirts to cover the evidence and begged him not to come out to his father.

I had done and heard the exact same thing. I had tried to kill myself but botched it on purpose at the last minute. When I met Gary, he had gotten sober and confronted all of his demons. The biggest was living openly and honestly, not allowing his life to be less than anyone else's. I was not out when Gary and I met. I had fake girlfriends. I lied to my family and friends. I had become an expert at hiding my true emotions. My father had taught me that. Gary would not stand for it.

When I told my mother that I was gay, one of the first things she said was that I could never tell my father.

"He won't understand. He won't ever talk to you again."

"That is not fair, Mother," I said. "To anyone. I have to tell him."

She began to yell, which stunned me. "You will force me to make a choice, Wade—you or your father."

"You're saying he won't accept me."

"I'm saying he won't know how to accept you."

I hung up and didn't speak to my mother for weeks. Out of the blue one day at work, I called my father.

"How 'bout them Cards?" he asked.

The Cardinals were having a good season. It was the Tony La Russa years, and the 1996 team would go on to win the NL Central and make it deep into the playoffs. My dad loved this Cards team because it was filled with history: an old Willie McGee, who returned to St. Louis to end his career, and a retiring Ozzie Smith.

"Old guys know how to lead," my dad said.

It seemed an ominous warning.

I told him I was gay.

He didn't respond.

"Did you hear me?" I asked.

"I heard you, boy. What kind of answer do you expect when you announce something like that?"

"How about 'I love you.'"

"Love ain't got nothin' to do with it." Pause. "Does your mother know?"

"Yes. I told her a few weeks ago. She asked me not to tell you yet."

"When the hell was everyone going to let me in on this secret?"

I told him about Gary.

"We helped you buy that house you're in, so don't do anything stupid," he said.

I went blind with rage, and he hung up.

The letter I received from him a few weeks later was ten pages long. My father never wrote a letter, birthday or holiday card in his life. The only thing he wrote was the name of a new stock into his ledger, or a list to remind my mom to buy him beer. I sat on my front porch and read the letter.

My father believed that I had been led "astray" by "older, practicing homosexuals."

I laughed at that. Gary was younger than I was, and I thought of him trying to obtain a license to practice his sexuality, much a like a doctor, dentist or a sixteen-year-old wanting to drive.

My father wrote that he could not imagine the life I'd "chosen" nor the lifetime of pain I would endure: the loss of friends, my job and God's grace. But most of all, family. He said that my life would be filled with darkness and hate. He wrote that he wanted nothing to do with me, much less Gary.

I showed Gary the letter when I walked inside. I cried, he held me and then I tucked that letter away in a storage bin in the back of my closet. I stacked shoes I rarely wore on top of it.

I promised myself it would be the last secret I ever buried.

The phone on the kitchen wall rang, knocking me from my thoughts. Gary turned to answer it.

"It's your father."

He held the phone out to me for what seemed like eternity, five seconds morphing into a minute. My legs were paralyzed. I was shaking.

I hadn't spoken to my father in over two years.

Gary shook the phone at me and then, without warning, dropped it. The phone twirled and then banged against the wall, over and over again.

"Oops," Gary said.

Gary refused to play games, be it baseball or life.

I stood, woozy, and picked up the phone. "Hello?" I could hear my dad saying. "Hello?"

"What do you want?" I asked.

"Can you believe it? Big Mac did it. How 'bout that? How 'bout those Cardinals?"

This was my father's apology.

I hung up.

The phone rang seconds later.

"Didn't think I'd ever live to see that again in my lifetime," he said in a rush.

He didn't say, *I didn't think I'd ever live to see my son again in my lifetime.*

"History in the making!" he blurted. His voice was slurred.

I didn't say a word.

"I miss seeing games with you," he continued.

I waited and I waited for something more.

Silence. So deafening I could hear the buzz of the ancient lights in our kitchen.

What should I do?

He had hurt me more than I knew was possible. How many holidays had I missed? How many times had I sneaked out of work and cried in my car at lunch? How long did I survive until the wound healed and scar tissue developed and I finally began to feel nothing at all?

Through the receiver, I could hear my mother nervously cleaning the kitchen in the background.

As a hospice nurse, my mom used to always tell me that nearly every person she cared for at the end of their life was filled with deep regret. She heard all their stories when the dying knew the end was finally near, when they were laced with morphine, when they could see God extending His hand to them. The dying regretted working too much, not enjoying life more, not spending enough time with family, not pursuing their dreams or taking chances. But mostly, my mom used to tell me, they regretted not forgiving those who had hurt them.

"You don't have to forgive *and* forget, Wade," she would say. "You can't rewrite your history. But you can put a period and start a new chapter. The one thing you don't want is to end your life filled with regret because it will eat away at the little time we are blessed with here on earth."

"How many homers do you think he'll hit before the season ends?" I finally asked my dad.

I heard a crash. Gary had dropped a bowl into the sink. He was staring at me.

"Seventy," my dad said, suddenly chipper. Silence. "You know," my dad continued, his voice shaky, "baseball's not a one-man game. Mac needed help. Takes a team. Can't go it alone."

And this, I knew, was his big apology.

When I hung up and turned toward Gary, he took the

spatula and flicked cream cheese frosting at me. It clung to my shirt for a second before rolling off in chunks.

"Nothing sticks to you!" he screamed. "How can you just shrug off two years of pain? Do you know how many times you woke me up crying in the middle of the night? Do you know how many times you called out for your father when you were having a nightmare? Do you remember how much anguish and hurt this has caused both of us? He cannot just pick up the phone, not apologize and have you take him back as though nothing happened."

"He's my dad," I said.

October 2015

"Is McGwire still playing?"

I look at my dad and then at the TV.

Adam Wainwright has taken over in the bottom of the fourth inning. He doesn't really look anything like Mark McGwire, save for some facial hair and his height, but my father has trouble distinguishing people now. He calls the caretakers "Geri," thinking they are my mom. He calls young men he sees "Todd," remembering my brother.

His memory, his history, is all muddled.

"No, he retired, remember?" I say. "Broke the record. Then he became the Cards' hitting coach for a few years."

"That's right, that's right," my dad says.

He doesn't remember, but he makes it sound as though he does.

"Need him now," he says. "In the lineup or on the bench. Too many damn strikeouts."

The Cards had threatened in the top of the fourth, putting two men on before the Cubs struck out three straight batters. Poof. Rally over.

"Big Mac," my dad says, shaking his head.

"Broke the record, remember?" I ask. "Against the Cubs, too. Remember?"

He looks at me, still shaking his head.

"In his final at-bat of the 1998 season, Big Mac became the first Major League Baseball player to hit seventy home runs in a season," I continue. "You called it. Remember?"

"Now, that was quite a year, wasn't it?"

He couldn't really remember that year.

Could he?

What few remember is that McGwire's record—just like the fall I forgave my father—will always have an asterisk.

McGwire later admitted to taking steroids off and on for a decade. Although the substance he took had been banned by the NFL and Olympics, it was not prohibited by Major League Baseball at the time. McGwire regretted using them, saying it was foolish and a mistake, and he apologized.

But time has a way of blurring the edges of history.

With Big Mac, Cards fans remember the summer he chased the record. We remember that September home-run at Busch. We remember the fireworks, his childlike reaction when his record-setting baseball was returned to him, lifting his son over his head, the cheers.

Is this right? Is it wrong?

I could hold a philosophical debate with you all day long. But when I think about it now, it still gives me goose-bumps. Sometimes, I'll remember a moment in sports—Ozzie Smith's walk-off home run against the Dodgers in Game 5 of the National League Division Series, Ricky

Proehl's catch against Tampa Bay to send the St. Louis Rams to the Super Bowl, Northwestern University's first NCAA basketball postseason tournament, the St. Louis Blues' first Stanley Cup, a friend's little boy getting his first T-ball hit and being so excited he doesn't know which way to run—and I will weep my eyes out.

I think my mom was right and wrong. You don't always have to forgive *and* forget. Sometimes you remember and reconcile. Sometimes you just choose to focus on the warmth of the fire and not how hard it was to get it started.

I've chosen to remember specific moments. It's not just how I've survived, it's how I've become the person I am.

I've gotten to see my father laugh. I've gotten to see him vulnerable. I've gotten to see him age. I will see him die. And I would not have been able to add this history to my life had I not chosen to view my history in a different way. It simply would have stopped, a path to nowhere, and what good would that have done me?

I chose continuation over closure.

My history, good and bad, sticks with me. It sticks in my craw and my gut. Most folks I know run from their past. Sometimes it's healthier that way. Certain memories are too awful to relive every day. People hurt us deeply, and our souls are forever sunburned. We spend thousands of dollars in therapy to understand why the people we love act the way they do, and why we become the people we are.

People can love you *and* still hurt you. They can give you everything they possibly can, and sometimes it's the equivalent of the last few dried summer beans plucked from a garden.

I've come to learn it's because that is all they have to give. It's all they were capable of growing. And you can choose to hate the love they've tried to provide—no matter how flawed, little or dried up it may be—or you can choose to understand how and why they love.

There's a map in my heart, you see, that was hand drawn long ago, and it leads home. The map is of the Ozarks. And it looks just like the one my dad drew when I was little and we'd head out on our Saturday road trips.

And when I go back and see the land that birthed me and the man who raised me, I see things others don't see, too.

I see beautiful bluffs and meandering creeks.

I see the history of the people who preceded me.

I see a lot of ghosts.

And they say, "Tell the boy 'bout what you went through," and "Don't you ever turn away from the hard."

I'd be a downright fool not to listen.

The Cubs go 1-2-3 against Wainwright, and I hope that history is on my side once again. Teams usually score the most runs in the middle innings of a game.

I look at my dad. He nods at me and then skews his eyes toward a giant oak in the yard, which is dropping big acorns on the roof yet still stubbornly holding on to all its leaves.

"Lotta history in that old tree, boy," he says.

I nod back. "There is, Dad. There is."

5TH INNING

"It Takes Teamwork"

October 2015

Where I am sitting right now, watching the fifth inning, is pretty much the exact location where my grandma Shipman's kitchen used to be located. The view is the same but completely different. The well-kept, tiny homes that once dotted this rural street are now in need of repair. Chain-link fences that keep barking dogs at bay and showcase rusting cars that will never be repaired have largely replaced cute flower gardens, shiny Buicks and sweet grandmas.

The kitchen has been replaced, too. My grandma's tiny kitchen, always a hundred degrees even in the middle of February, and its vintage appliances, Formica countertops, pink Formica and chrome dinette set, the black-and-white checkered floor, the mammoth bread box and wood recipe boxes have been replaced by a god-awful nondescript open concept.

My dad shakes his head as the Cards lineup strikes out, one batter after another.

I spent inordinate amounts of time with my grandma in her tiny kitchen. It was where I felt the safest. That kitchen was not only where my family gathered every Sunday and holiday but also where I learned to cook and bake, my grandma teaching me the history of our family through the food she made. Her kitchen wasn't just a place to cook; it was the place where she connected our family's past to the present. I had squirrel, possum, rabbit, fish and the best pies, cakes and cookies.

That kitchen is also where I shared my life with my grandma. After baking, she would always cut two slices of her beloved cherry chip cake, pour a cup of coffee for herself and a glass of milk for me, and we'd sit at the Formica table and talk, mostly about what I was going to do when I grew up, how I was going to change the world, see places she never had the chance to see.

"What do you think Paris is like in the spring?" she'd ask. "Send me a postcard when you go."

She'd continue, "My only dream is for you to have a better—and easier—life than I did."

I think of Northwestern University. What she did for me. What my father didn't.

The last Thanksgiving my grandma hosted was when I was in college. I returned home on break and spent most of my time in the kitchen with her, baking pies for the family. When we finished, she cut two slices, and poured a cup of coffee for herself and a glass of milk for me.

"Tell me about Chicago," she said, eyes wide, elbows on her Formica table.

My grandma's only demonstrative sign of ego was venting her pies with a signature *S* for Shipman.

★ ★ ★

"If I was manager, heads would roll!" my dad suddenly yells as yet another Cardinal strikes out. "I'd bench all them sons-a-bitches. They'd learn somethin' from your old man."

I look at my dad, shaking his head in disgust at the world as he always has, and I can feel lava flow in my gut.

He sees me watching him. He always knows when I am, even now, when he often doesn't know what time of day it is.

"Not enough teamwork," he says, continuing to shake his head. "They're good, but they ain't a team."

"They won a hundred games, Dad," I say.

"Molina got hurt," he says, his memory now clear as a bell, referring to the Cards catcher who injured his thumb in Game 3. "Lost all that personality. Cubs got all the damn personality now. Who'd'a thunk?"

There is no doubt that the newfangled Cubs are loaded with pizzazz: Dexter Fowler, Anthony Rizzo, Starlin Castro, David Ross, Jake Arrieta, manager Joe Maddon.

The Cards are certainly good but not oozing personality as in the past with the likes of Big Mac, Willie McGee, Ozzie Smith, Albert Pujols, the Mad Hungarian.

One of the main reasons my father has always loved the Cardinals so much is that the team is filled with history and characters.

Since the Cardinals were established in 1882, the team has boasted memorable players: Rogers Hornsby, Frankie Frisch, Dizzy Dean, the "Gashouse Gang," Stan Musial, Enos Slaughter and the "mad dash" to home plate, Bob

Gibson, Lou Brock, Whitey Herzog, Tony La Russa and so many more.

Every decade, the Cardinals seem to have a team defined by big characters.

"This team has lost all the energy. Lost all their heart." He looks at me. "You can just tell." He stops. "Team is family. Family is team."

He laughs and shakes his head yet again, but in a different way. "This family had personality. This family won more'n we lost, didn't we, boy?"

I don't answer.

He laughs again. "You can't say we were lackin' in personality, though, can you, boy?"

This time, I nod.

"I could never say that."

The 1970s and 1980s

Sports fans love to root for teams ripe with personality and history: the Yankees, Dodgers, Cowboys, Patriots, Celtics, Red Wings, Crimson Tide, Fighting Irish, Duke and North Carolina.

And then there are the teams that pull off the miracle: North Carolina State over Houston in the 1983 NCAA Basketball Championship; Team USA's gold medal in hockey over Russia in the 1980 Olympics; the Jets over the Colts in Super Bowl III.

These weren't the prettiest teams, nor the most balanced, but they were loaded with personality: Jim Valvano, Jim Craig, Joe Namath.

I would consider my family to be a part of this group. We weren't the prettiest, nor the most balanced by a long shot, but we did stick it out, and our team was rich with characters.

In fact, my father and mother were the biggest characters I've ever known. I couldn't write a novel with wackier protagonists. However, they essentially ruined my view of "normal:" a normal life, normal people, a normal world. They made it downright impossible for me to view the world as anything other than boring when they weren't a part of my team. It's a reason I fell in love with Gary: he matched their crazy with a pair of aces and three queens.

To understand my parents fully, you must first understand *I Love Lucy.* They were, in many ways, Fred and Ethel Mertz come to life. They tormented one another, like the purple martins that dive-bombed my Grandma Shipman when she'd hang out her laundry or pick tomatoes. Their relationship was built as much on mutual disrespect as respect.

Did they love each other?

I believe in every fiber of my soul they did.

Did they hurt each other?

I know in every fiber of my soul they did.

They enabled one another's dysfunction, and that would be their downfall.

To wit: Despite familial high cholesterol, my father ate like a man on death row. From a young age, he suffered an ongoing series of TIAs, or transient ischemic attacks. These brief interruptions of blood flow to the brain cause temporary stroke-like symptoms—such as weakness on one side of the body, vision problems and slurred speech—but are temporary and often resolve within twenty-four hours.

My father's face drooped like a wilted hydrangea when this would happen.

My mother, the nurse, would assess the situation quickly but could never convince him to go to the hospital.

"A beer and a shot of whiskey solves everything," he

would say, reaching for one, or both, with his good working hand and drinking from the good side of his face.

I would panic.

"There's nothing you can do," my mom would say, pouring him another.

She was no better. She "sneaked" cigarettes for decades.

"Only one or two a day," she would lie.

"Go have a cigarette," my dad would tell my mother when she was stressed or combative. "And bring me a beer on your way back."

The two battled and enabled one another like no other couple I've ever seen, save Fred and Ethel.

One Bloody Mary in the morning for a puff before breakfast. A stop at the party store to buy some booze and a pack of cigarettes. I'll spot you one TIA for a persistent cough.

And yet they could make each other laugh harder than anyone I've known, and they could both laugh at themselves, the trait I now consider to be the most important for survival.

My father had a wicked sense of humor. We played quickly off one another, too, like a shortstop to a second baseman pulling off a tricky double play.

My mother was usually the target.

I remember one summer morning after she had worked a night shift and driven to the cabin to spend the rest of the weekend with the family. She walked in, exhausted, shaking, and told us that she had nearly been in an accident on the way down.

"Are you okay, Mom?" I asked.

"Is the car okay, Geraldine?" my father asked.

She proceeded to tell an elaborate story about how she had screeched the brakes on a stretch of country road not far from the cabin to avoid hitting a turtle. Not any turtle, mind you, but one she said was "the size of a VW Bug."

My father started to laugh.

"That's a helluva turtle, Geraldine."

"Not only that," my mother continued, "but while I was stopped a big bobcat leaped from the side of a bluff and landed directly on top of the turtle."

She had barely finished before my father and I were on the floor. It started a decade of endless jokes, most of which involved my father and I buying stuffed animals and setting them in front of her car, a bobcat atop a turtle.

My best friends actually enjoyed my parents' company as much or more than mine.

How do I know?

They invited them to parties, sometimes without letting me know.

"We'll be seeing you Saturday for Susan's soiree!" my mother would announce the day before the party. "See you later!"

This started long ago.

My fraternity brothers invited my mom and dad to party with them during parents' weekend—sometimes without telling or inviting me—but they also officially voted them to be "more fun" than me one afternoon.

Then there was the glorious drunken tailgate prior to the Missouri Tigers winning a big football game in an upset when I was given a chair *outside* the circle next to the keg and my father was given my seat of honor. After the game, the fans in gold and black—always thirsty for a victory—rushed the field. I was cheering, high-fiving everyone around me when I realized I had been abandoned by my friends.

I looked around. Left, right and, finally, onto the field. There, in the throng, was my diminutive, drunken dad helping to knock over the goalposts and carry one out of the stadium. There was my dad hauling it to Harpo's, the bar everyone went to celebrate in Columbia after a game. And there was my father on the shoulders of college kids, who were carrying him around as if he'd just kicked the winning field goal himself.

My father drank for free that day.

In an effort to expand my parents' views and also to help them rekindle the romance in their relationship, I took them on elaborate trips—because I wanted my mother to experience luxury and pampering at some point in her life. One of my parents' dream trips was to Ireland. I planned the whole thing. We stayed in castles, saw the Cliffs of Moher, ringed the Ring of Kerry, took a boat to the Aran Islands, rode horses up sheep-strewn mountains and saw hidden magical lakes. On the overnight flight there, Gary and I ate dinner, brushed our teeth and—like most others—settled into our seats to sleep, knowing the next day we'd be working on fumes. The sound of cheers and youthful yells woke me and Gary at two in the morning.

"Stupid kids drinking the whole flight," I said.

I looked around. My father was in the middle of the aisle doing Jager shots with a group of Irish kids. When we landed, he was still drunk. The kids gave him a faux key to the country: a tin cutout from a can of Guinness they'd created with nail clippers. We stopped for breakfast. My father ordered a pint at a pub instead. They took his photo and hung it on the wall. We were only three hours into our trip.

As we drove through Ireland, I kept seeing my father eating something from his travel bag. I thought it was perhaps mints or crackers. It was the remains of a hoagie that he bought on their drive to St. Louis, packed in his suitcase and ate on the flight and now the trip. It was at least five days old. It had not been refrigerated.

"I don't think you want to end up in a hospital here, Dad," I said.

"Man has a gut like a goat," my mom said. "He could eat roadkill, belch and be fine."

They laughed as my father continued to munch.

They were a never-ending party.

Even at the holidays, my parents followed their own set of rules. On Christmas, they dressed as Mr. and Mrs. Claus, and my father would hand out cans of Hamms beer—even to children—and ask relatives if they wanted him to sing a rather risqué version of "Jingle Bells." On Thanksgiving, my mom would order the biggest box of wine she could find, and they would dribble out glasses of it the moment after the coffee ended. When I took Gary to his first Thanksgiving at my parents' house, he discovered just how they did things, including the fact my father liked to leave a fully stuffed turkey sitting out, unthawed, for hours, saying it needed to reach "room temp" before it could go into the oven.

"We're going to die," Gary mouthed to me, before dragging me upstairs to talk. "And is anyone even going to be sober enough to actually serve dinner, much less cook it?"

My father always had a drink going, beer to wine to hard liquor. He loved whiskey on the rocks, and the soundtrack of my childhood was of ice clinking in a cocktail glass beneath the glow of a faux gold touch lamp.

He always had a toothpick in his mouth, which he could twirl in a constant circle. My father cleaned his teeth constantly, sucking air through them, squeaking, squawking, whistling like a haunted goose. He would leave soggy, half-eaten toothpicks everywhere, a constant worry for my mother, who had taken our beagle numerous times to the vet to have them removed.

"How much wood can an old goat-witch chuck?" my mother would always sing to him.

My father was excellent at cards, be it bridge, canasta, poker or hearts. He was ruthless in his determination to win. He made children cry.

"You gotta learn the hard way," he'd say to a five-year-old. "You're either a winner or a loser. Life's tough."

My dad would wake at dawn when he would visit me and begin to smoke ribs, chicken and turkey on my tiny back deck in St. Louis. "Invite all your friends," he'd say. "Get a keg!"

He and my mother were incredible cooks.

They bought one of those mammoth sets of world cookbooks in the 1970s and made their way through nearly every recipe, be it from Greece, Spain, Italy, Mexico or Ethiopia. This despite the fact that the international aisle of their grocery store consisted mostly of refried beans, olives and pasta.

But my friends never saw my parents' troubled side. They never could see my dad was a chameleon, an actor, a true switch hitter.

Why are most funny people funny? Because they're sad down deep. They're troubled inside. Humor is a way to deflect attention. It's a way to ingratiate people. It's a way to have others forgive your faults.

I know, because my father's humor was mine. I was his son, inside and out.

We could turn on a dime. But we saved our most vicious humor for one another. Soon the jokes started to go too far.

One day in the car when I was visiting my dad, he took me for a "Sunday drive." Like in the past, we drove around the dying towns in which he'd grown up and pretended as though they were still vibrant. He did not seem to notice the boarded-up storefronts, the people with confederate flags flapping off the backs of their broken-down pickups or the trailers near-collapse on concrete blocks.

I began to ask how he felt about all this. His shoulders got rigid as he drove. His face turned beet red.

"Wanna hear a joke, boy?" he asked. "How do you turn a fruit into a vegetable? AIDS."

"That's not funny, Dad," I said.

"You've turned into a fuckin' liberal," he said. "Be tough. It's just a joke."

"That's not a joke, Dad. That's offensive and mean. I

have friends who have died of AIDS. I know people who are living with it. It was ignored by our country for years. My people were left to die. You can't joke about that."

"*Your* people?" he hissed at me. "Livin' in the city has changed you."

I slammed my fist on the glove box.

"Pull the car over now."

I got out. I waited for him to apologize.

He pulled away, leaving me to cross the bridge where my brother was killed and walk the few miles back home. When I got back, he had made me a drink. He considered it an apology. I was too emotionally exhausted to drive the five hours home. I took the drink, slammed it and retreated to bed at five in the evening.

"Laugh it off, boy!" he yelled.

For much of our lives, we did laugh it off. We laughed at one another and laughed off the other's faults as eccentricities. We treated each other as a fan might a team that had become a loveable loser, like the Cubs had for pretty much the entirety of their existence. There was something more appealing and palpable about treating each other this way rather than actually giving voice to our issues with one another.

The danger with this behavior is it becomes truth. We began to see each other too often as jokes and not real people. We used punchlines, rather than fists, to inflict damage on the most vulnerable part of ourselves. Bruises on your soul never heal. They leave scar tissue. Like Chicagoans, who never expected the Cubs to win many games during a season—much less win a World Series—my dad and I never expected each other to change either.

That was wrong.

And we didn't realize until it wasn't funny anymore.

Until we couldn't laugh at one another any longer.

Summer 2009

I discovered a box of condoms hidden in my father's bathroom cabinet the week after my mother died.

I hadn't been snooping. I had been cleaning the house that hadn't been cleaned since my mother fell ill of cancer over a year earlier.

My father had been telling me a dirty joke as I bleached the kitchen sink. When I didn't laugh, he picked up a bottle of Windex, shot it at me and said, "I wish I could make you disappear."

Whenever I tried to help my father, he viewed it as an end-around: I was attempting to sabotage him, hurt him, playing a game. I was trying to outmaneuver and outsmart, like inserting a leftie to pitch to a pinch hitter.

I took my cleaning supplies and retreated to my parents' bedroom and bathroom. When I saw the condoms, I simply dropped the scrub brush I was holding into the trash can.

My parents' bathroom was filthy.

But my father?

I must be insane, I thought. *What was I getting wrong here? These couldn't be his.*

I took a hard seat on the cracking tile in their bathroom, which my father had originally designed in the 1970s. The wallpaper was filled with *Saturday Evening Post* covers of Normal Rockwell illustrations: boys and their dogs, kids in school, families saluting the flag.

I looked around the bathroom. This was how my father always viewed the world: the happiest times were long gone. America—after his childhood—was flawed, wrong and headed into the gutter.

It must have been an odd struggle, a jarring juxtaposition for my father: perpetually striving to recreate *Happy Days* in a world that he knew was quickly moving forward. Without him.

Perhaps that was why he had always drank a bit too much. Joked a bit too much.

I stared at the box of condoms I was still holding.

Or was it all because, it suddenly hit me, my father had never been happy?

He was always a bit of a mystery, the chemical engineer and logistical human who measured, calculated, weighed everything, even emotion. The older he got, the more he disappeared on weekends to play golf, or fish with friends. Even when our family was spending time at the cabin, he would simply leave in the morning and return late in the evening.

"I need to get the mail, run the trash home, pick up some beer," he would say.

I never thought much about it. He was *so* routine—down to what he ate and said—that it seemed normal.

A staunch Republican, he was always agitated at the state of America. He lived in fear: everyone was going to hell. The world was going to hell. He never understood why his brother and sister left the Ozarks. He was angry my aunt bought a cottage in Michigan, that my uncle bought a boat in Florida. No one should spend their money; it was not to be enjoyed, it was to be hoarded.

My mom talked many times of leaving my father, divorcing him and starting anew, something I always dismissed as a part of her charming wackiness.

"Sure, Mom," I would say. "Uh-huh."

"I should leave him," she would say in her syrupy Ozarks accent. "The old goat-witch."

I always thought my mother was just being like many mothers of a certain age. She liked to complain about her husband, like so many of the Ozarks nurses she worked alongside. It was normal, as natural as the mosquitos and oak trees.

But maybe, I now thought, I should have listened. Maybe I had been deeply misogynistic.

She hinted at his dark side, that he was not the image he portrayed, that the 1950s *Leave It to Beaver* father he claimed to personify was, in fact, a bit more Hitchcockian in nature.

Over the years, my father's drinking had escalated. He had never been a cleaner. That had been left to my mom. And then to a woman who had come twice a month until my mother got sick and my father decided he didn't want to pay her. My mom was too weak to fight anymore.

That was my father's MO. A man who garnered money by refusing to spend any of it. *Everything* was frivolous. Even a clean toilet.

I looked again at the box of condoms.

I had been in here cleaning, perched under my father's sink, pitching moldy Speed Sticks and broken bottles of Old Spice. The sink, thick with beard shavings, had gotten clogged, begun to leak, and mold was growing in the wooden cabinet below.

I am not handy. I have trouble changing a lightbulb. But when I am determined and angry, I can stop a semi from hitting a turtle in the middle of the road.

I think of my mom and dad, turtles and bobcats, but this time I don't laugh.

These were not ancient condoms, perhaps squirreled away by my brother some three decades earlier. The design wasn't from the 1970s, or even '80s. There was no picture of Ron Jeremy.

I opened the box. Most of the condoms had been used.

I read the cover: "Ribbed for her pleasure."

My stomach lurched.

There was a receipt stuffed inside.

May 2009.

They had not only been purchased recently, but while my mother was dying, bedridden, no longer able to walk.

I started crying. It just hit me, like a sudden thunderstorm. I was furious, thinking of my mother.

And then, just as suddenly, I stopped.

I got up and began to hunt through his closet and drawers, under the bed and mattress, in old shoe boxes and jacket pockets. Nothing.

My head was spinning, and I was so angry, I couldn't see straight. I turned his bedroom upside down.

Nothing.

I returned to cleaning, my mind still whirling. A few hours later, as I was cleaning their bedroom and putting it back into some sense of normalcy again, I wiped down and polished my mother's old wooden jewelry box, the one that had a carved G for Geraldine on the top. I popped it open.

More condoms. Sitting atop her beloved pearls.

There was another receipt inside, this one recent, too.

Gary came in, and I dragged him into the bathroom and showed him.

He held me as I cried.

"This isn't new behavior," he said. "Remember the cabin?"

I had laughed that memory off, too.

My parents had built a new cabin on a different creek after I graduated from college. The lot overlooked the water, which rushed over a dam just downstream, but it was across from an island that jutted out into the river and served as a campground. Revelers jammed the site in the summer. My father loved it. He partied with campers every night, dancing on the deck to their music, trying to toss them beers across the water, whooping it up with strangers.

One early evening, after way too many drinks, my father tripped and fell in the bathroom. He screamed, and we found him lying on the floor. His head, on first inspection, looked fine. We then saw a geyser of blood flowing from his chin. I thought he was dead.

"My tooth," he finally said. "Find my tooth."

My mother kept an entire cabinet stocked with hospital-quality disinfectants and bandages. Then she found a needle, which she held under a lighter, along with some white thread, and began to put a few stitches in his chin.

"I should have used purple thread, you old goat-witch," she said.

"Find my tooth, boy," my dad yelled at me. "I can't afford a new one."

He smiled in a cartoonish manner and showed off his smile. A prominent tooth in the front was missing.

Gary, not yet fully understanding the ways of the Rouse House, looked at me, his face etched in panic, as I began crawling around on the floor to find my father's tooth.

"Maybe you could use our insurance," Gary suggested.

I looked up at him and shook my head. "Just find it," I pleaded.

Gary bent over and scoured the bathroom for a few minutes before walking back to the sink. He looked at my dad and asked, "Where are your tools?"

Gary had figured it out. My father had gone down like a house of cards, and his temporary cap, which had turned permanent a year ago when he refused to return to the dentist, had popped out of his mouth, into the air and down the drain.

My mom ushered my father into the kitchen to soothe his injury with ibuprofen and whiskey, and Gary took apart the drain like MacGyver.

"This is totally hot," I told him. "I thought gnomes lived under the sink and delivered our water."

In the crook of the pipe was my father's tooth. Gary delivered it like a minion to a king: on a bath towel as if it were a crown.

My father stood and hugged Gary, a gesture that stunned us all.

"Saved me a fortune!"

And then my father popped the cap back into his mouth without cleaning or sterilizing it.

"Nothing will kill him," my mom told Gary. "Old goat-witch."

We returned to reassemble the sink. Gary was perched on his rear, angled into the cabinet, when I heard him groan.

"Are you okay?" I asked.

Like a magician, his hand appeared from nowhere. His fingers gripped an old box. I took it from him.

Condoms.

Gary looked up at me.

"What the hell?" he mouthed.

"Whose are these?" I asked.

"How would I know? Are they your brother's, maybe?"

"No, Todd died long before this cabin was built." I looked at him. "They can't be my mom's." I stopped. "They couldn't be my dad's." I stopped again. "Could they?"

I looked at the box. The condoms were old. They had been hidden for a while. I did the math in my head, from when the cabin was built to now. I thought of how many times my father disappeared during weekends. How often he played golf less than a mile from here. The bathroom spun. I heard footsteps.

"Put them back," I said, tossing the box back to Gary. "Where they were."

"Are you sure?" he asked.

"Hide them," I said. "Like we do everything in this family."

The sound of my father popping another beer downstairs jolts me from the memory.

Part of me wanted to run downstairs and hit him. Part of me wanted to throw these boxes of condoms in his face and scream, "What in the hell has been going on all these years?" And part of me simply wanted to ignore the situation, which usually worked best with my father.

These could not be his, right? There had to be some other explanation.

I marched downstairs, Gary following closely. My fists were clenched. As Gary once pointed out, I was gay Bob Dole, my hands constantly clenched into a fist, or around a pen. I was—like my father—a master of containing my rage, I had learned.

"Wanna watch *Happy Days* with me?" my father asked, sipping a whiskey, the now-faulty gold touch lamp flashing on and off with every jerky move my father made. "Comes on right after *Gunsmoke*."

I weighed my options.

The last time my father and I had a serious conversation, I told him I was gay and he refused to talk to me for two years. When I battled with him over the direction of my mother's cancer treatment, he said, "She wants to die." And when I told him I was quitting my job to write full time, he said, "Don't expect any inheritance."

Why was I still here? Why was I still in his life?

Somewhere, deep down, I knew he loved me. But I wasn't ever sure that he liked me.

These happy days are yours and mine…

As the theme song played, my father smiled, and I thought of what my mother, the longtime hospice nurse, had told me as she lay dying.

"Some people will never know themselves. And some people will never let anyone know them. Your father is both. He can't provide unconditional love. Only love, under his conditions."

I spent the final days and weeks with my mom, postponing much of my book tour to be with her.

Our family and her nursing friends surrounded her, but my father was rarely there. He would stop in for a few minutes at a time, shake her leg and say, "Get better, sweetie. See you soon!" And then he would rush off to get the mail.

"Don't be angry at him," she told me. "He can't handle this."

My overwhelming grief kept me from making it an issue.

When my mom's dear friends would visit, I would often leave the room so they could have their final moments with my mom. I heard one of my mother's dearest friends—a nurse and true force of nature—whisper to her, "You've forgiven him, right? Before you go, you have forgiveness?"

And then one time, "He didn't deserve you, for all that he put you through."

In the throes of cancer, she would again tell me, "I should have left him. I should have left him."

"Why?" I would ask.

"You don't need to know."

But in her last weeks, when she was on hospice and loads of morphine, she would talk to herself when I was alone with her late at night, words, snippets of conversations dropped like breadcrumbs leading nowhere. They came rushing back to me once again.

"That woman!"

"The fog on the car window!"

"My babies! Stay for my babies!"

"She's in my house!"

In piecemeal, I didn't understand, blaming the morphine, but now, had they formed a lifetime of shouting that went unheard? I was haunted by the ghost of a man I never knew.

Who was my father?

Fonzie knocked me from my thoughts. My father laughed and stood to go pee and snag another drink.

Maybe I did know my father. And perhaps that was why I'd long kept so much distance, moving to St. Louis and then to Michigan.

I've always believed that one of the greatest gifts we can receive is to know our parents and grandparents as people, as flesh and blood fuck-ups and humans, just like us. For one, this allows us to stop revering them, to take them off that pedestal that we tend to leave our parents on, and to see them face-to-face. For another, I believe it allows us to live for ourselves, to stop pantomiming life in order to make those parental mirages happy.

I looked up at all the framed photos of my life and my family, snapshots of the past in dusty frames.

My band concerts. My plays. My college honors and inductions. My high school graduation.

My dad not in a one.

Why did my mother stay?

Had she created her own version of *Happy Days* to survive?

As I heard my dad tinkling, the bathroom door wide open, I thought of when I came out to my father, of the chilling letters he wrote me that nearly destroyed our relationship.

"I came out because I hadn't wanted to lie," I had written him. "I wanted to live in the light. I wanted to love."

"You should have kept it all a secret," he wrote back. "Hidden from the world."

And I continued to remain a secret from many I loved because of him. My father returned, another drink in hand.

What had I learned from my dad?

To lie? To keep secrets? That you only receive love when you meet certain conditions?

Perhaps that was why I had been alone and miserable for the first thirty-one years of my life.

Suddenly, I stood and went to his sacred rolltop desk in the living room. I yanked off a humidity-curled Post-it whose adhesive had seen better days. I found one of his beloved fancy pens, the ones he used to meticulously detail his finances in leather-bound ledgers, the kind Mr. Potter used in *It's A Wonderful Life.*

"I have no secrets," I wrote. "How about you?"

Perhaps it was childish, perhaps my anger got the best of me, perhaps it was passive-aggressive and I should have talked to him man-to-man to get the truth instead of leaving it all a mystery, but I walked upstairs, put the note on top of the two boxes of condoms and returned them to my mother's jewelry box, but not before sticking her strand of pearls in my pocket.

I didn't regret it. Not one piece of it.

The next time I visited, the condoms, and note, were gone.

And, as was my father's routine, he never spoke of it.

October 2015

Adam Wainwright is mowing down the Cubs in the bottom of the fifth inning. The game is half over.

I look at my dad and then at the TV. In life, my father is old. In baseball, Adam Wainwright, nearing thirty-five, is downright ancient.

I like to think that I am still middle-aged, but I am not, unless the median lifespan for an American male has suddenly jumped to a hundred years old.

Wainwright is tough. So is my dad.

So am I.

Wainwright is a character. So is my dad. So was my mother.

So am I.

I think of my mom and my dad, our little team. I think of my father's character flaws, and why my mom stuck it out with him.

Love? Teamwork? Codependence?

Or are all of those things really the same?

Strangely—or perhaps, *sadly* is a better word to use—my

love for my father didn't vanish even after finding those boxes of condoms. I will never know for sure if they were his; I still like to imagine there must be some other explanation, and they were not. Either way, unfortunately, my respect for him diminished, and that seemed so much worse.

I look around this house, where I used to sit with my grandma in her kitchen.

When I returned to move my father out of our childhood home—a too-big house whose steps he could no longer navigate—my father refused, so I used all the lessons he had taught me. I lied and said we wouldn't sell it. I told him I would continue to be there for him but only *if* he moved.

It made me sick to do that, but it worked.

That's the thing about *conditional* love. It's a contract signed by an unwilling party who has no other choice. The one with the upper hand always decides when and how much love needs to be given.

In the years that followed, I was there for my dad, despite our history and character flaws, until the end—wiping him, reading to him, sharing my life with him—because that's the thing about *unconditional* love, the lesson my mother, the hospice nurse, taught me: you love, without any conditions.

How many gravel roads did my mother travel to care for strangers who had little money or love in their lives? How many times did she share these strangers' stories with me so that someone in this world would hear about them— that their lives had mattered despite the hardship—before they were forgotten? She demonstrated unconditional love to me, and that didn't just change me, it saved me.

How many gravel roads did I travel until I met Gary?

Like me, he willingly accepted love with conditions from everyone because he felt he wasn't worthy of the real thing. And when we're taught to love with conditions, we constantly add clauses to the contracts in our lives: I will allow you to speak to me that way because I deserve it. I will take this job and be paid less than anyone else because I am less than. I will be surrounded by people who put me down rather than build me up. I will even love myself in fractions of a whole because I have so little respect for who I am and what I deserve.

When you meet people who love you and support you with every fiber of their being, you become lit from within.

The light shimmers through the windows, and I can see dust motes dance.

My mother used to say dust motes existed to show us our place in the world. I didn't really understand what she meant until I got older, but I finally figured out her parable: we are nothing really, in the big scheme of things, just little motes floating around the universe. Most of us are invisible, unnoticed, until the light shines upon us, into us, through us, and makes us bright.

Finally visible.

There was nothing more magical growing up than an Ozarks summer filled with lightning bugs. Some kids used to capture them in mason jars, but I thought that was just downright cruel. I used to lay back on the edge of the bluff by the cabin, my feet dangling over the side, and watch the lightning bugs. Some, I realized, flashed only once, while some were like the stoplight going into town, blinking constantly.

But all had such short lives, a few weeks in the summer, so why—I always thought—shouldn't we flash our light like crazy while we had the chance?

But too few of us ever do.

Unconditional love. Sounds so simple and yet it is the hardest lesson to learn in life.

But it is a gift, especially as years pass, and you build your own life, one filled with mutual respect and no secrets, no regrets, nothing hidden anywhere in your house or your soul.

6TH INNING

"The Comeback"

October 2015

Against all odds, the Cardinals are making a comeback.

After two singles and two strikeouts, Tony Cruz doubles. The Cards cut the lead to one and have two men on base.

The Cards bench is alive. The Cubs faithful are roaring for the last out. My dad is acting like he always has. Although the best is happening, he sees only the worst. He sees only the past.

"At least they don't have Tony the Tinkerer," my dad yells, mind suddenly clear, referring to the Cards' former manager, Tony La Russa.

"Haven't for a while," I say.

"Good," he says. "Won't screw things up."

Tony the Tinkerer.

Wade the Wrecker.

Everyone screws everything up for my father.

In many ways, I considered myself to be the Tony La Russa in my father's life.

He both loved and hated the Hall of Famer who was the Cardinals' longest and most winning manager in history.

He won two World Series championships with the Cards, and the team was perennially in the postseason with him at the helm.

Although the team and the manager were proven winners, my father viewed them as constant disappointments.

My father believed they should have won the World Series *every* year, and anything less was a failure. Moreover, Tony's teams showed that baseball was—like the world—changing, and there was nothing more unnerving to my father than that.

I believe my father saw the end of his reign in me and Tony because we dared tinker with the way things were. We had the audacity to test tradition. We opted not to do things the same ol' way in either baseball or life.

La Russa changed the game of baseball profoundly. He studied statistics, often relying more on percentages than his gut. He was a master statistician who scrutinized hitter-pitcher matchups. He yanked relievers after facing one batter—often just one pitch—and would put utility players in the lineup over everyday starters simply because stats showed they had demonstrated success against a certain opposing pitcher. La Russa changed the way baseball used and viewed "closers," saving his stopper for the ninth inning only, a practice now universally implemented.

He also considered himself as valuable a member of the team as any of its players, believing there was always something he could do to give them an advantage or help them win.

His constant tinkering infuriated my father. Ironically, the way he managed should have impressed him if you stop to think about it. My father was an engineer. Calculations, percentages, formulas were his life. He could recite the periodic table of elements as easily as he could calculate in his head the payment on a thirty-year, $217,000 mortgage with 4.25 percent interest (including taxes and insurance).

Moreover, he never followed his gut. He followed the numbers, be it in career or money. *Safe* numbers: A four to six percent return in the stock market was amazing. A five percent increase in your salary when you switched jobs was astronomical. A two percent raise every year was lovely.

I tinkered and cobbled and played the percentages my whole life. And then I decided to blow things up.

And, like La Russa, I am winning.

Just not in my father's eyes.

I glance at him.

I never will.

Which is why I haven't told him.

My first novel recently sold. At auction. And rights have already been sold in about ten foreign countries. At auction.

In publishing, that's huge. In an author's life, that's celebratory if not life-changing.

After publishing four humorous memoirs, and then struggling and failing to sell another, this is my first book to sell in over half a decade. I am now a novelist. I am back in the game. Big time. Ring the bells: the Cardinals and Wade Rouse—just like Dolly Levi—are staging a comeback.

But my father doesn't know this. Because I don't want him to know. I don't need an ounce of his indifference, a penny of his money or a snort of his indignity.

I did it, all on my own, with the entire world against me.

I don't want him to know because this is mine and mine alone, and I don't want my father to steal any of my joy for the first time in my life.

The times I have been honest with my father have not gone well. The times I have trusted my gut were the times I lost. The times I expected a different outcome, the game changed on a dime.

So, like La Russa, I have once again analyzed the matchup and my odds of winning.

The percentages say, "Don't tell your father a damn thing."

"Who'd have thought the Cards had it in them," my father says, looking directly at me. "I had 'em pegged as dead. Losers."

I glance at my dad once again. "You have to be willing to believe in your talent, work hard, keep grinding, never give up, put your back into it…believe that anything is possible."

As if on cue, his eyes wander to the sad bookshelf he has underneath his oversize TV. It is filled with biographies of Churchill and Reagan, mysteries and Sudoku.

My previous books may live in homes, libraries, bookstores and schools across the US, and they will soon publish in Germany, Italy and Spain, but they do not and will never dwell in my dad's house. The answer to one of the clues in his childish crossword puzzle books will never spell out my name.

December 1983

When I told my father I was majoring in communications, it was over Christmas break of my freshman year. My grades were coming in the mail. I knew he would get them first when he went to the post office. I knew he would open them before they ever made it to me.

He had made it clear: straight As. Nothing less was acceptable. Not after turning down a full ride to the local community college and blowing his money on a "liberal arts" college, words he could say with such disdain you felt as if you had stabbed him in the back and ran away with his wallet.

He was preparing prime rib, which he liked beyond rare—"I like it to 'moo' when I slice it"—and his wineglass was full again. I remember his face being flushed from the heat of the kitchen, the red wine and—forgive me for the gross misreading of the situation—the warmth of family.

I had entered college and declared a major in business just to please my father. I hated it. So much so that a couple of weeks into my first semester, I changed my core classes.

I'd had an English and lit professor who was so taken with my work that he wanted to move me into an advanced class for freshmen.

"Why didn't you sign up for honors English?" he asked.

I had no clue it existed.

I told him my mother had served as my college counselor. I told him where I grew up. I told him that for most of my classmates, graduating high school was the apex of their educational pyramid. I told him my father had wanted me to go to school at a local community college, and if I were to go to a four-year school, then business was the only way to make a living.

"You got one of those, too?" he laughed. He looked at me. "You got a life, too, that's separate from his. That's why you're here. Remember that."

"I changed majors, Dad," I told my father that Christmas. "To communications."

I saw his body grow stiff. I saw his hands clench into fists. Just as mine do to this day.

"How in the fuck do you make a livin' communicatin', boy?" he said in a whisper barely audible over the hum of the oven and the holiday music.

"I like writing," I said. "I like books. I always have."

"I, I, I," my father said. "Well, *I* don't give a damn what you like."

Suddenly, he turned and tossed the carving knife he was holding in my direction. It spun and stuck into the side of the trash compactor, an ironic placeholder for his actions. I knew he never meant to hurt me. I truly did. I just knew he wanted to make a point that would stick forever.

He had not wanted me to go to Drury College, a private liberal arts school in Springfield, Missouri, where my mother had earned her nursing degree. He had wanted me to go to the local community college, where I'd gotten a full ride scholarship and where I could—I guess—nurture my interests in livestock. He had gone to the School of Mines, a prestigious engineering-focused university in Rolla, Missouri. My mother had insisted I go to Drury.

"Why would our son have a lesser education than you received?" my mom asked my father.

That had ended the conversation about Drury, but not about the financial impact. So I applied for every possible scholarship I could to lessen the financial blow to my father. I had also left for college despite the fact that I didn't want to leave my mom alone after my brother's death.

"If you don't move on with your life, then I can't either," she told me the summer before I left for college. "If you're happy, I'm happy."

I never saw her cry, until she was pulling away in the car after helping me move into my dorm. Her shoulders were slumped, her body heaving.

"The world centers on communication," I told my father that Christmas, pulling the knife free from the trash compactor and handing it back to him as casually as if I were passing him the butter. "I'm good at it. It's what I was meant to do."

"I was meant to be a prince, too, boy. Didn't work out that way." He looked at me, the blade of the knife out. "Life don't work out that way. When in the hell are you ever gonna get that through that thick skull'a yours? Damn optimist. The world ain't what you think it is."

I got all As. He found that out when he opened my grades the next week. He never said a word to me about it. I would graduate magna cum laude with honors in communication. I would minor in Spanish. A more shameful combination my father couldn't imagine unless I were to order a mai tai and coconut shrimp at his favorite steakhouse.

That is, until I applied to graduate school.

My advisor in college, the one who had encouraged me to write, pressed me to apply to graduate school. I was certain I would *not* be admitted. I was certain I didn't have the talent, much less the connections.

I had zero confidence, although I had gotten into a wonderful fraternity, made incredible friends and had—despite hiding my sexuality—an incredibly fun and transformative college experience.

I began to research colleges early my senior year and settled on two: the University of Missouri and the University of Kansas, both of which had fine graduate journalism programs. I visited both, thanks to college friends. However, in further research, I had come across Northwestern University, not only one of the nation's best universities but also one of the world's finest journalism schools. I asked my advisor, and he smiled, saying he was happy I had come to that conclusion. However, some of my peers were not.

"You will never gain admission to Northwestern," one told me. "No one does, except the very best." His silence after that said everything.

I was stunned. *Who says that?*

But it emboldened me. Whenever someone told me I couldn't do something, I set my mind to do it.

It was a long application process, including lots of recommendations, and taking the GRE. But the admission process mostly centered on writing. When I sent off my application, I got drunk with my friends.

I was accepted to Mizzou and Kansas, but I never heard from Northwestern.

I wasn't even rejected.

I became angry as my senior year came to an end. At first I thought the process might just take a while longer, but then I began to accuse fraternity brothers who lived in our house of throwing away my letter. These were tactics I had learned from my father: everyone is out to get you.

Just a few days before graduation, I called the Northwestern admissions office and left a message.

I graduated and returned home. Kansas and Missouri were awaiting decisions.

One weekday morning—the first full week I was back home after graduating college, the week before I was to start my job at a local newspaper, the phone rang. It was the admission office at Northwestern.

"We sent a letter," the woman said. "Congratulations! You were accepted."

"Really? Thank you! But I never received the letter," I said. "Where did you send it?"

I heard shuffling.

"We mailed it to your home address. We often worry that college mail gets lost."

"How strange. It must have gotten misplaced somehow."

"We called, too. Spoke to someone…" More shuffling. "A note here says it was your father. He said you had declined acceptance."

The world spun. My eyes filled with tears. "What? No. That can't be. I want to attend. It's my dream."

"We gave your spot away." She stopped. "We can put you on a waitlist. Or you can defer to another semester."

"Please" was the only thing I could say, besides, "Thank you."

I drove directly to the hospital to talk to my mother in person.

She had no idea. She was working in ICU at the time, and her reaction to my pronouncement was the same as her dealing with a patient who had coded: calm, emotionless, in charge.

"I will handle this," she said.

My father acted as if this had simply slipped his memory.

"I was sorta thinkin' you shouldn't go to graduate school."

"You were sorta thinkin'?" I screamed.

"You had four fuckin' years of college, boy. Paid for by ME! You need to get a job and be a real man. You don't need to sit your fat ass in an ivory tower talkin' 'bout how you're gonna fuckin' change the world." I remember him glaring at me and popping open a beer. "World don't change, boy. You do. Startin' now."

A few days later I received a call to tell me a spot had opened, and I would be joining the fall class.

"Gravy train is over, you spoiled piece 'a shit!" he yelled, storming out of the house. "I will not pay a penny for this nonsense."

Door slam. Garage door creaking open. Truck peeling out.

"Don't worry about it, honey," my mom said. "I'm paying for it. Your dreams are my dreams."

The generosity and privilege of having my entire education paid for me by my parents can never be underestimated. It allowed me to enter the world and workforce not only debt-free but also in a place of financial strength too few ever know. And a piece of me understood my father's reaction: graduating college to him and my mother was the ultimate dream. My grandparents' change changed my family's life. And attaining a master's degree made no sense—logical or financial—to him. He did not understand fully the impact Northwestern would have on my life and career.

My father never visited me in Chicago, but my mom and two grandmothers—one of whom was riddled with cancer and would die just a few months later, both of whom had never ventured much beyond a city larger than Joplin—would move me into my apartment and walk the campus.

"You go here," my grandma had said, neither as an exclamation or as a question, but as both, an affirmation that I had extended the dream she had begun for my mother.

My world changed at Northwestern. I was challenged. I was part of a diverse world at school and in Chicago. I went from using a typewriter to a Mac. I interviewed with Hearst. I interviewed with Crain's. Before I left, I had written a feature for the *Chicago Reader*, interviewed with the independent paper and was on course to become a writer for them.

My father had other plans.

"One of my company's trucks will be comin' through Chicago next week," he told me over the phone the day after I'd graduated. It was the first time I'd spoken to him in months. "Your lease is up. Pack your crap up. Be ready to go when the driver gets there. I'm payin' him extra to help you load."

"But, Dad… I have a job…"

"A job that don't pay shit."

"I'm not leaving Chicago."

"You will be on the truck, boy. And you will come home. End of story." He stopped. "See how good I communicate."

When I got home, my father greeted me in the driveway.

"You got a month, boy," he said. No hug. No "Welcome home, son!" No "Congratulations!" He could not let his guard down for one second to take pride in what I had accomplished. "One month to find a job that pays a decent wage round here. I don't give a shit what it is. You got an education now. But you ain't got no work ethic."

No work ethic?

I grew up in rural America. I had fought every step of the way. I had just earned a master's degree from Northwestern. I had a job lined up.

The one thing I had learned from my father and all of my elders was to work hard. Harder than anyone else. To put my back into it when I wanted to give up.

I stood in that driveway and looked around the woods

that had served as a playground for me growing up. This was where I would find a mattress of ferns and lay down and read for hours, traveling to places I never dreamed I would visit. This was where I would find a sassafras whose trunk was curved just so and lean against it beneath a slant of light, writing in my little journal, making sense of my life, my family and the world. When I was forced to hunt, I would retreat to these woods so my father couldn't find me. I swung from grape vines off banks over spring-swollen tributaries here, outrunning boys who had wanted to beat me up. And way out in these woods, where a stand of oaks held homemade targets my brother had made, was where he taught me how to use a shotgun.

"Not to shoot at any critters," my brother had said, seemingly seeing a future where he was no longer with me, seemingly understanding me better than I thought a country boy could ever know his brother. "But at someone. Ya know, if ya ever needed to. Square in the eyes. So they know ya mean business." He shook me hard again. "You gotta learn to fight for yourself. When somethin's comin' at ya, ya gotta take that shot. Or you're the one who dies."

I looked around. There was still a tunnel in the brush behind the house where I used to have to run down the baseball when it would roll into the woods. It has stayed the same after all these years.

And then it hit me, staring at that tunnel. I knew the game my father was playing because we played it so long ago. He wanted me here. Home. With him. Trapped in the past, so he's not alone.

Forcing me to return was the only way he could make that happen.

My anger turned to sadness.

I heard the creak of a floorboard in the second story. I didn't look up. I knew my father was watching me. When you stood at the window overlooking the driveway and woods in the upstairs TV room, the floorboards moaned, like an old ship at sea. I used to think—when I'd stand there to watch the sunset and dream about my life—that those floorboards mirrored the sound of my soul.

I knew the game I now had to play.

I woke early and drove to the library every single morning. I scanned the want ads in the *St. Louis Post-Dispatch*. I secretly cut out the jobs from the paper and stashed them in my wallet, before crafting letters and mailing them with my résumé.

At night, I came home and watched the Cardinals with my father as if nothing was going on. The team was slogging through a miserable, sub-.500 season, and my father raged for hours at their inconsistency.

"This is just like the good ol' days, right, boy?" he would ask me, so happy and so angry at the same time.

The phone rang a few weeks later. It was from the editor of the *St. Louis Business Journal*, who wanted to talk to me about a job.

"Should we tell Dad?" I asked my mom.

"No, he left me at my lowest," she said, referencing his abandonment decades earlier after Todd had died, not understanding what I had learned about him at the baseball game we attended. "The least I can do is return the favor."

And off we went, the two of us, to St. Louis. My mother
waited for me on the riverfront while I interviewed.

"I got the job!" I yelled when I saw her.

My job was to help comprise the paper's annual Book of
Lists, which detailed the city's top companies and nonprofits
in different categories. I would also be a part-time reporter.

When we returned home, I told my father I had gotten
a job, under his deadline but in St. Louis.

"Last time your mother or I help you," he said.

"I don't need your help," I said.

"At least you're coverin' business. Maybe you can finally
learn a thing or two about how to make a dime."

Before I left, my grandma Shipman and mom in tow to
help me move once again, my father stood in the driveway
and said, "At least you're livin' someplace where I can go
to a game now. Congratulations, boy! You've now made
one good gol'damn decision in your life."

I lived in St. Louis for nearly twenty years. I kept changing jobs to move up and make more money, but—in retro-
spect—it was really to gain my father's approval. I worked in
public relations for Washington University's School of Engineering, which my father loved to chide me for—"You're
doing the poor man's work for a rich man's world"—and
then for a number of prestigious private schools and colleges.

I met Gary, came out but also dipped into depression. I
loved Gary, but I didn't like my life. I was chasing prestigious jobs I didn't want. I was tired of working for someone else. I was living in regret.

"I want to write a book," I kept saying.

One Sunday night when I said that—as the *60 Minutes* clock ticked off the seconds until another workweek began—Gary looked at me and said, "You know how much I hated the sound of that stopwatch every Sunday night? It was literally counting down the seconds until I had to go back to school and get the crap beaten out of me. I vowed I would never feel like I was trapped in my life again. I vowed I would never hate the passage of time. It's too precious."

I looked at him.

"Just write a book, Wade! Stop talking about your dreams and start making them come true. I support you fully. You need to hear that. But you also need to hear that you and only you can make it happen. And you can. You are barely tapping your talent. Write that book. Change your life. Let's have an adventure. I believe in you."

I woke every day at 4:00 a.m. I transformed the minuscule space we called a back porch in the city into my writing studio. I wrote for two hours in the dark, worked out for one and got to work by eight. Most nights, I worked late due to endless committee meetings. Ironically, I began to train for my first marathon at this time. Writing a book and training for a marathon became inseparable in my life. I could not see any progress until I fully committed myself to both. I didn't think I could ever write a decent chapter much less run five miles, but then you do, and you think, "What else is possible? How much further can I push myself?" And that chapter becomes a hundred pages, and those five miles turn into fifteen, and then you think, "I can actually do this." It's cumulative.

I ran my first marathon in the time I had set for myself:

under three-and-a-half hours and under seven-and-a-half minutes a mile. I completed my memoir in 2004 and sent queries to literary agents on New Year's Eve. Two weeks later, I had seven offers to read my full manuscript. Another two weeks later, I had three offers of representation. Another couple of weeks later, my memoir had sold to Dutton.

That's when I decided to quit my job to write full time and move from St. Louis to Saugatuck, Michigan, the resort town Gary and I had fallen in love with.

When I quit my job, a former coworker told me, "You will not make it. You will end up coming back here and begging to have your job back. And we won't give it to you."

It was a gut punch.

But I looked at that person and said, "You don't know me very well, do you?"

When I told my father, he said, "You will not make it. You will end up comin' to me and beggin' for money. And I won't give it to you."

And I looked at him and said, "You still don't know me very well, do you?"

But we were both right. There would come a time when I needed him, and he would not give me any help. And yet I still persevered.

And there would come a time when he would need me, and I would be there to help him. And he persevered.

We too often forget in life that we are not preordained to play only one specific role like ballplayers do: defensive shortstop, designated hitter, power-hitting cleanup man, set-up pitcher, closer.

We are sons, fathers, husbands, friends. We are wives, mothers, sisters, aunts, caregivers.

We are human.

And sometimes we forget that in order to survive.

But you always have to believe that there is a comeback in your future.

October 2015

The Cards' Brandon Moss hits a line drive single to right field. Peralta scores to tie the game, and Cruz races toward home.

I stand, yelling.

My father sits up in his chair.

"Out!" the home plate umpire signals.

Inning over. Game tied 4–4.

"Stupid, stupid, stupid!" my father yells.

He shakes his head.

"We're all tied up," I say. "They're making a comeback."

October 2011

"I'm going to bed."

"What?"

I stood, folded the blanket and grabbed my pillow. Gary looked up at me from the couch.

It was Game 6 of the 2011 World Series, and the Cardinals' goose was cooked.

The Texas Rangers were up, three games to two, and leading the Cards 7-5 in the top of the ninth.

It seemed hopeless. The Rangers had called in their ace, flame-throwing closer Neftali Feliz. The Cards' first batter had already struck out.

One out, bottom of the ninth.

Game over. Season over. Nightmare year over. Career over.

"You never give up on the Cards," Gary said.

"Good night."

I headed into the bedroom just around the corner from our tiny TV room in the knotty pine cottage in Michigan where we lived. I turned off the light and crawled into bed.

"Mabel!" I yelled to our shaggy mutt, the one who never left my side.

"She's not giving up either!" Gary yelled.

"Traitors," I said to the sheets.

The TV continued to blare. Joe Buck's voice. I leaned over, slammed the door and pulled the pillow over my head.

This season, this series, this game, this year has been among the worst of my life.

The Cards shouldn't even have made the playoffs, much less made it to the World Series. Just a few weeks ago, at the end of August, the team was barely over .500 and had only a minuscule chance of even reaching the postseason. But they made an improbable September comeback, going 23-9 over their last thirty-two games to erase a 10.5 game lead by the Atlanta Braves, who lost their regular season finale to allow the Cardinals to make the playoffs.

The Cards faced the heavily favored Philadelphia Phillies in the National League Division Series. The series was razor close and made national headlines for the appearance of the "Rally Squirrel" at Busch Stadium, which zipped across the field in Game 3 and then again in Game 4, when it ran directly across home plate as a Cards player was batting. The Cards were ahead 3-2 at the time and held on for a 5-3 victory, with many Cardinals fans claiming the squirrel was a good-luck omen. The Cards defeated the Phillies 1-0 in Game 5 behind a masterful Chris Carpenter three-hit shutout. They then beat the Brewers in six games to reach the World Series.

But now against Texas, the talented team destined to finally win a title, the Cards seem to have met their match.

Me, too.

I think of the Cards' year, and I think of mine. I have nearly killed myself trying to save my father and my career. I have tried for an improbable comeback. And I have lost. My father has won.

After selling four memoirs and editing an anthology—two of which had come out in 2011—I couldn't sell a book to save my life. My publisher had disbanded the imprint I'd been with for my last three books. My editor and publisher—the ones who had long loved, supported, championed, believed in and bought my work—were gone. Now I was adrift, and the editors my agent had reached out to had either not loved my new book or my old sales numbers enough to take a chance on me. I'd pitched other ideas, from new memoirs to self-help books, and I'd talked to countless editors, but nothing.

My life had gone down the shitter, literally.

Gary was cleaning toilets. After leaving his sales job to help me full-time, believing things were finally taking off, he had now been forced to take a job at a local bed-and-breakfast, where he mostly made the meals and scrubbed the bathrooms.

I was humiliated.

"I'll do anything to extend the runway," Gary said, over and over, about making enough money until I could sell another book. "Until your next book sells. I believe in you."

His belief was unwarranted.

I was taking on any freelance gig I could grab while teaching writing workshops every couple of weeks. I was speaking at schools and local libraries for fifty bucks a pop. We were scraping together a few hundred dollars here and there to pay our mortgage, our bills, our groceries. I refused to touch my savings. I had an exit strategy: I would go six months off of my savings, if need be, and then find a full-time job again.

I pulled the pillow down tighter over my head.

I cannot see any light at the end of this tunnel.

Four books in five years, coverage in *USA TODAY*, the *Washington Post*, Chelsea Lately, NPR, and my writing career was already over. In the blink of an eye.

My mind turned to my mom.

She always said, "Life is as short as one blink of God's eye."

What we do with that blink, she constantly reminded me, was up to each and every one of us, because that defined our legacy and whether we had honored the unique gifts and voice that God had given us.

I could feel my eyelid scraping the pillowcase.

Scritch. Scritch. Scritch.

I had never given up in my life. Why now?

Was I just exhausted of trying? Had my dad worn me down? Or was he right? Was it time to grow the hell up and realize that some dreams just didn't come true?

I blamed my father for much of my downfall that year.

A polar vortex had gripped the Great Lakes right when my fourth humor memoir was published. Much of my book tour was canceled due to the record cold. I tried to persevere. I arrived in Chicago—in the midst of snow and windchills well south of zero—for a much-anticipated interview on WGN. In advance of my segment, which was to promote my tour stops in Chicago, the meteorologist told viewers to stay home and not to venture outside. "For anything," he said.

The segment was then tossed to me.

Moreover, my beloved dog, Marge, the eighty-five-pound rescue mutt who literally rescued me from my depression after coming out to my father, had been diagnosed with cancer at the age of thirteen and was only given a few months to live. She would die in the spring.

I continued in a deep funk over the loss of my mother in the summer of 2009.

And my father was becoming increasingly unhinged. His agitation with me had escalated into screaming and cursing. He was calling me more than a Robocall on speed-dial.

"You just called, Dad," I would say after picking up five minutes after he'd hung up. "Is everything okay?"

"You fuckin' piece of shit. How dare you talk to me like that."

A half hour later, I would answer again.

"Too good to call your old man?"

And again.

"Why did you leave me?"

Often, his voice was slurred, his stories outrageous. People were out to get him, even kill him. Who? I would ask. Everyone, he would say.

I was exhausted and concerned. I was answering his call every hour on the hour. I was trying to cobble together enough cash to stem the tide. I was trying to write another memoir, but creatively nothing was coming and professionally I had to ask myself if another memoir would even sell. I called many of my father's longtime friends. He was no longer talking to, reaching out or seeing them. When they tried, he did not respond.

I had been invited to attend a mega-author book club and author festival in the south. I decided to stop and spend a few days with my father on the way there.

On the last hour of my drive, my father called my cell no less than a dozen times. He was angry, agitated, screaming. "Where the fuck are you, boy?"

"Almost there," I said. "It's a ten-hour drive, remember? And we've already ordered a pizza to pick up so you can eat when we get there. We'll be there soon."

"Fuck you," he said, hanging up.

He called a couple of minutes later, saying nearly the same thing again.

By the time we got there, my father was passed out on the living room floor, a freshly made whiskey on the rocks sitting on the end table. I thought he was dead. Gary and I sat him up, cleaned him with a washcloth, made him drink little gulps of water and, when his eyes were fully opened, fed him torn pieces of pizza, before hauling him up the stairs to bed. When we started to seat him on his mattress, I nearly collapsed. His bed was covered in waste.

We stripped his sheets, remade his bed, bathed him and started the laundry.

He was passed out, snoring, which relieved my anxiety just enough for me to start snooping. I found a bottle of OxyContin sitting on the bathroom counter. I found another in what had once been my mother's makeup drawer.

And yet another in my bathroom. And another next to his meds in the cabinet over the coffeemaker. I studied the labels. He had squirrelled away enough OxyContin to stun an elephant.

"Dementia, drinking and pills are not a way to cope with anything," I told him the next morning.

Amazingly, he was still up at six in the morning. He was groggy but his routine remained intact. Down to his refusal to admit anything was wrong.

"I know you miss Mom. I do, too," I said. "But you need to move on with your life in some way. We need to move you out of this big house. Why don't you move up next to us?"

"I am not movin' from this house!" he said. "Ever."

"Dad, we thought you were dead when we arrived. Do you even remember last night?"

No answer.

"We had to haul you upstairs to bed, which was covered in your own filth. There is no railing on the stairs. What if you fell? There is no downstairs bedroom. This no longer makes sense."

"You left me! You have no say in the matter!"

"Dad, I left home in 1983. That was nearly thirty years ago. It's time for a change. This house is filled with wonderful memories, but it's filled with a lot of ghosts, too. You need a new start."

I called the hospital and made an appointment. I was not allowed to be with my father while the exam took place. I was finally told that he was fine, that he was simply lonely.

"Don't you get that?" a staffer told me. "His wife is gone. His son is dead."

My eyes widened. "I'm still here. And my father is not well. He's drinking excessively, more than he ever has. I found Oxy everywhere. I know he has dementia and his health is poor. His lungs rattle when he sleeps."

"You hear all of that over the phone when you call?"

I was about to come unglued.

"This is absolutely none of your business, but I asked my father to move to Michigan with me a hundred times. My father wouldn't do that. I can't get him to move to a smaller home."

"Why should he be the one doing all of that?" I was told. "You're the one who left him."

My head began to spin. In the eyes of my father and the Ozarks folk where I grew up, it was shameful to leave. You stayed where you were born. You lived by the bluffs, rose to the sounds of fish breaking water at dawn. You were baptized in the creek. The rocky terrain absorbed your tears and blood.

My father and his friends were fierce protectors of a certain way of life. But if I had stayed where I grew up, I would be dead.

I spent the next two days watching reruns of *Gunsmoke* as my father got drunk.

It was bitterly cold. My father refused to turn on the heat.

"I have an electric blanket," he told me when I asked if I could turn it on.

I started a fire and slept on the couch in front of it. I

woke in the middle of the night, my side in pain. I showed Gary the next morning.

"I think it's a spider bite," he said.

I felt as if I were getting sick. The day before we were to leave, I turned on the shower, which had not been updated since the house was built in the mid-70s. Water barely trickled from it. It was lukewarm. I undressed and looked in the mirror at my spider bite. My entire side looked like it had been burned. There was a red comma-shaped series of blisters running along my side. I could barely move.

I texted a picture to a friend who was a nurse.

Shingles, she texted back. Are you stressed?

Are you serious? I texted back.

We were leaving the next morning. I could not even call in a prescription, so Gary drove the entire way, and I sat up straight in the car in agonizing pain. Moreover, the event we were attending was a spectacle, meaning authors dressed up for events. I was going as Evel Kneivel one night and a 1980s prom girl the next. I went to my events, returned to my room exhausted, got dressed up to entertain the troops and returned to my room to collapse. I didn't shower or sleep due to the pain.

My father called every hour on the hour, asking if I were ever going to come and see him.

On our drive home, I could hear my father coughing through the phone. He sounded bad.

We had just made it home when I knew it was serious. I asked a nursing friend of my mother's to check on him. She called back and said he needed to go to the hospital. I turned around and made it back just as he was hospitalized for pneumonia. He was so ill, his lungs had to be peeled, just like the skin off an orange. He went through detox while in the hospital, pulling out tubes, climbing over the back of the bed, trying to jump out the window, cursing at nurses and doctors.

My father entered a rehab facility after his hospitalization, and it was there I convinced him to sell our family home.

In the attic, between old furniture, ancient tools and forgotten memories, I found boxes filled with my grandmothers' heirlooms. Charm bracelets, recipe boxes lined with recipe cards of my family's favorites written in my grandmas' signature lettering, hope chests stuffed with quilts, family Bibles, scrapbooks, McCoy vases and desert rose dishes.

I found my next book: a novel inspired by my grandmothers' charm bracelets and how their memories connect a family that has forgotten its history.

I knew it was the right idea for a novel, but I also knew that it would take time not only to write but also perfect. A man writing women's fiction under his grandmother's pen name seemed akin to a literary *Victor/Victoria*.

I started it that day, sitting in the hot attic on the floor writing ideas on the top of one of the cardboard boxes, overwhelmed by the memories from my childhood.

I spent an inordinate amount of time with my grandmothers growing up: Sundays in their kitchens watching them bake, evenings in their sewing rooms watching them take scraps and turn them into beautiful quilts, Saturdays at the beauty parlor watching them get their hair "did" and sharing stories with their friends they never told when the menfolk were around, and summers at our log cabin. My grandmothers were both volunteers at the local library, and they were always reading and inspired my love of books and writing. "You can go anywhere and be anyone you dream when you read," they told me. "All it takes is imagination."

Over time, I got to know my grandmothers not just as my grandmas but as real women, who had loved and lost, dreamed and hoped, been knocked down by life and gotten up with grace, hope and strength to soldier on time and again.

One of my grandma Shipman's biggest pleasures was "the simple things," like watching the sun set over the creek at our cabin every summer night.

I was inspired to write novels meant to serve as tributes to family and our elders as well as to inspire hope and remind readers of what's most important in life: each other.

I wanted to write characters in my novels who were reflections of my grandmothers and my mother: good, kind women who are knocked down over and over again by life but stand up, dust themselves off and soldier on with grace and strength, women who are too often overlooked in life and literature.

I told my agent, "If a reader walks into a library or bookstore a hundred years from now—long after I'm gone—and picks up one of my novels, says my grandmother's name, understands the person she was and the sacrifices she made and, perhaps, reconnects with their own family history to understand how they came to be, then my work will be done and my 'blink' will have mattered."

Sitting in the attic, looking at these boxes of heirlooms, I finally realized that my grandmothers—all of my elders—

were never poor. In fact, they were the richest people I'd ever known in my life, because they understood what mattered most in the world.

I knew, in my heart, I could do this. I knew it because my dad did, too, because he was raised by the same people. Our history wasn't just in our blood, it was engrained in our souls, and, like the red clay in the Ozarks, that never washed away.

I also knew I had to take the time to get it right.

I had enough money saved to go for about six more months. I knew I could earn enough money to go another six if I had to, but I would likely need at least two years to get this right. I also knew my father would not assist me. You don't ask a man who tossed you out of his trust to trust you with a loan.

After I had helped my father pack and move, I left and drove ten hours back home. I pulled over on the side of the road outside of Springfield, Missouri, to check on Marge. I reached back, petted her big ol' head, and she sighed. I rolled down the windows and listened to the bullfrogs moan, the sounds of my childhood, my Ozarks orchestra. But through it all, I heard my mother. I would often ride with my mom on her hospice appointments when I'd visit. It was a way for us to talk and get ice cream cones at the Dairy Queen on hazy summer days. Many of the people for whom she cared were dirt poor. They had been born and would die in the same house, just like their parents did. My mom provided prayer and palliative care, but mostly she just listened to them talk. She heard their life stories.

"Most people die with regret," my mom would tell me

as we drove in her old car over dusty Ozarks roads. "They regret not traveling more. They regret not doing the things they dreamed of doing." She would look over at me and say, "Promise you won't live with regret."

"I promise," I'd always reply.

I heard my mom that night, and I made two promises: that I would work as hard as my grandparents had taught me, and I would succeed beyond my wildest dreams.

From the side of the road, I emailed a Facebook friend who worked for *People* magazine. She had written a wonderful review of one of my books and had suggested—since I use so many cultural, pop and celebrity references in my books—that I would be a perfect person to write for *People*. She responded almost immediately, putting me in touch with her editor. It was a long, torturous interview process—complete with writing tests and timed deadlines, taking me back to graduate school at Northwestern—but I got the job, writing for People.com and covering breaking celebrity news.

Just as I had done writing my first memoir, I woke at 4:00 a.m. to begin writing my novel. I started writing for *People* at 6:00 a.m. I often worked sixteen hours a day, including weekends. In the evenings, I would write freelance articles for magazines and online publications. Every few weeks, I taught a writing workshop at a bookstore or library across the Midwest. Every few months, I taught a three-day intensive workshop for promising writers.

I was half-asleep, remembering all of this, when I heard a muffled yelp. I removed the pillow from my head.

"Get in here now!" Gary screamed.

I crawled out of bed and opened the door just in time to hear Gary say, "Are you watching? Wake up! Now!"

I walked into the TV room. The Cards fans were roaring at Busch.

"What happened?"

"The kinda hot guy everybody loves and is sad might leave is up to bat."

This was Gary pretending to be a sports fan.

"Albert Pujols?"

Gary shrugged.

I took a seat on the edge of the couch. There was one out in the bottom of the ninth. In what could have been his last at-bat as a Cardinal, Pujols doubled. Feliz walked Lance Berkman. Craig struck out. David Freese stepped to the plate.

Freese, a young Cards player who grew up in St. Louis and was a lifelong Cardinals fan, had been projected to have a breakout season until he fractured his hand. As a result, he had endured an unexpectedly tough year.

In the blink of an eye, Freese went down in the count, one ball and two strikes.

I shut my eyes and said a prayer.

When I opened them, Gary was looking at me.

"I knew it, Mr. Tough Guy," he said. "You never give up hope. Ever."

Freese connected with a ball and hit it well into right field. At first, it looked as if Rangers outfielder Nelson Cruz had a beat on it. He drifted back to the right field wall, but the ball kept sailing. It flew over his glove and off the wall.

Two runs scored, and Freese slid into third base. The game was tied again, 7-7. The crowd was roaring. I was screaming. The game went into extra innings.

But then in the top of the tenth, Josh Hamilton hit a booming home run—with one hand—to give the Rangers a 9-7 lead and—once again, it seemed—the series.

This time, however, I did not budge from the couch.

In the bottom of the tenth, the Cards pushed across a run to cut the lead to one but were again down to their last strike with Lance Berkman at bat. With a 2-2 count, he singled to right center to tie the game.

I stood on the couch, screaming. Mabel was barking. She joined me, jumping up and down on the cushions.

My heart was beating so quickly, the TV was spinning.

The game remained tied into the bottom of the eleventh. David Freese once again stepped to the plate.

He couldn't do it again, could he?

Freese smashed the ball to dead center. It soared out of the park.

"We will see you tomorrow night!" Joe Buck said, mimicking what his father always said when the Cards won a game in dramatic fashion.

There was going to be a Game 7. There was going to be a comeback.

I began to cry. So hard I couldn't see.

I grabbed Gary, and we jumped up and down and up and down, our little house rocking as if we were right there in Busch Stadium.

My cell rang. I picked it up without looking, thinking one of my friends from St. Louis was calling.

"Can you believe it?" I yelled.

"Still a game to go."

It was my father.

"Why are you calling me?"

"I called to thank Gary for waking me up to watch the rest of the game," he said. "I'd given up hope."

I glared at Gary. "You called my father?" I mouthed.

"You always give up hope," I said to my dad. "This was a miracle."

He laughed at my ironic choice of words.

"Maybe," my dad said. "Maybe."

I didn't know what else to say. I started to hit End on my cell, but stopped.

"Cards went through too much to lose now," I said. *Just like me.* "It's over. They'll win tomorrow night."

"We'll see," my dad said. "We'll see."

"They got it," I said. "Nothing can stop them."

"We'll see," he said again.

I shook my head.

"World Series champions," I said. "Who would have thought?"

"Game to go, boy," he grunted before hanging up.

I looked at Gary.

"Why? Why did you call him?"

He shrugged and batted his eyes.

"Why did he call you?" he asked.

"I don't understand what you're asking, or why you did this. I can't have him in my life any longer. It's toxic to me, to us, to everything."

"I called him because we all need to believe in miracles."

Gary looked at me. "We have to believe in those things we love." He stopped. "The Cardinals are going to win it all, I can tell."

"Have you become a sports fan?" I asked.

"I'm just a fan of yours," he said. "And you're going to win it all, too."

The Cards won the World Series in one of the greatest comebacks of all time.

And then my book sold.

October 2015

With two outs and one big swing of the bat, Anthony Rizzo homers, and the Cubs are back on top 5-4 in the bottom of the sixth.

My father rages.

"Losers!" my dad yells, looking at the TV and then at me. "Now tell me all about that gol'damn comeback, boy!"

I shut my eyes, seeking some semblance of peace, and think of Gary's father, somewhere in Carbondale, Illinois, watching the same game right now.

The first time I sat down to watch a Cardinals game with my father-in-law, George, his jaw dropped.

Gary was not a sports fan. He would ask how many outs there were when I was watching a football game, or how many touchdowns a team had scored when I was watching baseball. George expected the same of me.

When a Cardinal pitcher swung at a pitch rather than attempt to advance a runner on first with a bat, George wondered why.

"He has a .270 batting average against lefties," I said.

George looked at me as if J-Lo had suddenly appeared in his living room and was going to recreate her Super Bowl halftime show just for him.

When a Cardinals outfielder misplayed a ball in the outfield, I began to rant. George looked at me and said, "Mistakes happen. Yelling at someone who makes one never makes them feel better or erases what happens. It just embeds that negativity and usually causes future impairments in judgment. We're a team here, good and bad."

I nearly broke my neck doing a double take at him.

Gary's father was a superintendent. He coached sports, including baseball, much of his life. He was a taskmaster, but, at heart, he was a deeply sensitive man. Quiet, unassuming, calm.

My experience watching baseball with him was like viewing Earth from a different planet. He didn't yell. He was always level-headed and supportive. We watched hundreds of games together, and, in many ways, he became a surrogate father. One summer day, many, many years later, after I'd published a few books, we were watching a Cards game when La Russa was manager. The windows were open in their den, and the curtains—ones Gary's grandma had made decades earlier, featuring vintage deer romping in turquoise woods—were bobbing in the wind. He looked at me and said, "I'm very proud of you."

George was now in his eighties. He had battled Parkinson's for nearly twenty years. He had trouble standing and walking. Watching him eat dinner was akin to watching someone try to eat soup in the middle of an earthquake.

And yet he never complained, or raged, or quit. He was gracious.

"Did you hear me?" he asked.

"Why?"

"Why what?"

"Why are you proud of me?"

George cocked his head like the blue jay that kept watch from the fence. He looked at me for the longest time. "That's not a question you're supposed to ask, young man."

"What am I supposed to say, then?"

"Thank you."

It was then I saw a little tear trailing down his face.

I was not used to praise from a father figure. I was not used to someone like him being proud of me or saying he was proud of me. It wasn't embarrassing. It just seemed inauthentic.

Why would he say that? What did he want? What would follow to pull the rug from underneath such a compliment?

"Aren't you proud of yourself?" he asked.

"No," I said. "I'm not."

He began to tell me of his life for the first time: growing up destitute, a father who drank too much, working every possible job from the time he was a boy—gathering eggs to sell, delivering newspapers, lifeguard, construction—in order to save money to achieve his dream of going to college. The week he was to leave for school, he went to the local bank to retrieve his savings. It had already been taken.

George never returned home. He left for college, immediately secured two jobs—doing lawn care and maintenance for the college as well as doing construction in his off-hours—and also walked onto the football team and the track team. He went on to earn his master's degree and doctorate in education, and he became a superintendent.

"Growing up, I wasn't expected to be anything, and yet I became everything I dreamed," he told me that day. "And I believe that drove me to success."

I looked at him.

"Most kids would have been crushed," he continued. "They would've given up. They would've walked out of the bank, gotten drunk, beaten up a stranger or someone in their own family, but I didn't. I got the hell out of town and never looked back. And as soon as I did, my world changed. The world wasn't like the one my father saw. Yours isn't either. That pain drove us to succeed. And I think that's a rare gift. Because no matter the hell the world rained down on us after that—the hardships that bring most people to their knees—well, it sorta just felt like a soft shower after all we endured. Wade, our pasts made us able to forge our futures. We've done things many people only dream of doing. The students I've helped will continue this message. Your books will live forever." George stopped. "Look at me, Wade. Really look at me."

I turned and stared him right in the eye.

"Don't you see? It's not ever good enough for you because you've done all the things your father dreamed of doing. *You* got the hell outta Dodge. *You* were the entrepreneur. *You* call your own shots. And that's why you will never get his praise. But that's not on you. That's on him."

I began to cry.

"My money for college was taken, but that just made me

realize the safe was already empty," George said. "Don't you see? Didn't matter. Nobody could steal my dreams."

"How did you make it?"

"By picturing moments like this," he said.

George willed himself out of his rocker and slowly made his way over to me. He opened his arms. I stood. He hugged me.

We sat back down to watch the game. The Cards were losing but coming back strong in the middle innings.

"You know," George said, "the greatest comebacks are the ones we make in our own lives. Could be getting sober. Finding love. Being happy. Fishing on a Tuesday. Watching a game with your son-in-law. Not too many of us get back to even. Damn few come out on top. Those are the comebacks that nobody ever talks about."

My father roars at the TV, snapping me from this memory.

The Cards record the last out and close the inning. It's only a one-run game, but my dad says, "Too late now. Too late for any comeback. The die's already been cast, boy. Don't wanna talk about this shit show no longer."

I think of 1985.

My father refused to talk about my life or career much like he steadfastly refused to talk about the 1985 World Series.

It was a topic never to be broached.

Many folks believe that Missouri is a state evenly divided between the St. Louis Cardinals and the Kansas City Royals. That's not true. The state is—pardon the appropriate political pun—largely red, largely because of the team's long, rich history. Older generations grew up with the Cardinals and had nearly a century of history before the Kansas City Royals started as an expansion team in 1969.

The 1985 World Series between the Cards and the Royals, however, became akin to a divided state at war. My father and I, of course, both shot off our mouths, assuring a Cards win. It was all but guaranteed, too. Game 6. Cards up three games to two. Bottom of the ninth. Cards leading 1-0. The Royals leadoff hitter hits a slow roller to first. First baseman Jack Clark tosses the ball to pitcher Todd Worrell, who was covering the base. In what came to be known as "the call," Don Denkinger called the hitter safe, although it was clear on replay that the runner was out by a half step. The Royals went on to win Game 6 2-1, and crush the Cards 11-0 in Game 7 to take the Series.

My father's white pickup was covered in blue—posters, streamers, ribbon, Royals logos—and my fraternity room looked as if a Smurf dwelled in it.

Of course, fans of both sides viewed the result very differently. Royals fans said the Cards still had a chance but got their butts whooped. Cards fans feel as if the series was stolen from them. I feel that way, too. Yes, there was still a Game 7, but what the Royals fans forget is that a team is made of individuals, and once each spirit is broken, it can't be repaired overnight. I've seen a horse go down on the racetrack, and—in addition to the collective heartbreak those watching experience and feel—we also know that the end has come, right here and now, before our very eyes. We are silent, we pray, we mourn, but sports teams aren't like that. They don't just go down like that. It's a slow-motion fall. You can see they're broken, and you know it's over before the game even starts, but they still have to play the game.

My heart still breaks for that '85 team. Because I know how they must have felt: always a half-step away from their dream.

My eyes wander to my father's little bookshelf, and I think of George and what he told me.

No matter the hell the world rained down on us after that—the hardships that bring most people to their knees—well, it sorta just felt like a soft shower after all we endured.

Ironically, in my career as an author, that lesson has been the most important. My father was the stubbornest man I've ever known. People say the same thing of me. And I take it as a compliment, for it is strength, toughness, resilience that sets me apart.

I wasn't just equipped for rejection, I relished it. It was a badge of honor.

Hate me, I think. *Try to hurt me. Try to kill my dream. Try to end my career. I'll come back, time and again.*

Truly, career rejection never crushed me. I welcomed criticism because at least it showed interest in what I was doing. And it seemed like a soft shower rather than a torrential downpour.

Over the years, much of the literary criticism and rejection I've endured has centered on my show of emotion in my writing. I was too "touchy-feely" for many East Coast critics and literary bigwigs. "Too emotional," they would say. "Dial it back. Heart on the sleeve doesn't work for smart readers."

But I didn't dial it back. Because I couldn't.

Who are these people? I thought. *If you can't show your emotions in your art, then when can you?*

I can only bury so much, before a vine emerges. Either I tend to it or it overtakes me.

How do these emotionless critics and artists deal with the grief and disappointment in their own lives?

I finally realized it was all pretend. They were acting. They pretended they didn't care. They pretended they didn't have emotions. They weren't literary heroes. They were literary liars. They wanted people to believe that they were something they weren't: Strong. Invincible. Uncaring.

But that's exactly how the most vulnerable act, you see. As if they don't care. As if human emotions don't apply to them. I learned that from my father.

You can't fool me.

But you can only stage a comeback when you realize that you're operating from behind in some way. That doesn't mean it deters you, defeats you or demeans you.

It simply sets you up for great things in your next inning.

7ᵀᴴ INNING

"The Perfect Teammate"

October 2015

Matt Carpenter strikes out to open the seventh inning. The living room is quiet, a contrast to the mob scene in Chicago.

"Where's Racer?" my dad asks.

I look at him. Racer is the beagle we had when I was little. He's been dead for decades.

"I think he went outside to potty," I lie.

"What about Squeaky?"

My parents' cat. Long gone.

"Probably cornering a mouse," I say.

My dad laughs.

"Then get ol' Charlie in here on my lap," he says. "I need a distraction."

"Sleeping on the bed upstairs," I say. "You know how he loves to take over your warm spot when you leave the bed."

"Damn dog," he says. "Where's Gary?"

My father can detect when my mood has shifted. He can also tell when I'm no longer responsive to his rants. He wants a foil. He needs a companion. He needs a buffer.

"Gary!" I yell.

Gary emerges from the bedroom where the overnight home care worker usually stays. We have delayed her arrival until the game is over, so we could all spend "quality time" together.

"How long do these games go?" Gary groans, flopping on the couch with a copy of *Midwest Living*. He opens it to an article on pumpkins. "Did you know you can stack them to make them resemble topiaries in garden urns? My life feels brand new again."

My father shakes his head at Gary. For the longest time, my father has seemed to view Gary as either a rainbow-colored unicorn come to life, or as the new Ethel to his Fred, a replacement for my mom.

Ironically, it was my father's love—and respect—for my husband which reminded me that people—like a baseball game—can evolve when you least expect it. His transformation and his capacity to change, accept and love Gary kept me believing in miracles.

"You're somethin'," he says to Gary, shaking his head. "Tell me a story. Game's over. My boy's a glutton for punishment."

The irony is not lost on Gary. He looks at me and smiles.

"Well," Gary starts, "I'm not the storyteller, your son is."

I kick Gary so hard, the magazine falls from his lap.

"Tell my father a story," I say, the sentence drenched in an alternative meaning: *Just save my ass for a second please. Give me a break. You've been hiding all day. I've been engaged in mortal combat disguised as a baseball game.*

"Okay," Gary says. "Did I ever tell you the story of how I met your son?"

I look at him. He's told everyone this story—his family, strangers on the street, baristas, cows—but my father has never stayed long enough to hear the whole thing. He no longer has a choice.

My father looks at Gary and grunts. You can tell he regrets his decision asking Gary to join us.

"Good," Gary says. "I didn't think so."

Back in the mid '90s—before the era of cell phones—I was having a bite to eat with a friend and some caffeine before hitting the bars in St. Louis. I was newly out—literally a couple of months—and my life revolved around making up for all the days I had lost.

"Are you two dating?"

I looked up and Hugh Grant was standing at our table. Gary had Hugh hair—big, full, high—and he was very, very Day-Glo tan. He was sporting jean shorts, rolled high, boots and a white crop top much like Wham! might have worn.

"Do you two even know each other?" I asked my friend.

"Yes," he said. "And, no, Gary, we're not dating. This is Wade."

"Thank God," he said, taking a seat, uninvited at our table. "There's new meat on the menu!"

I stared at him.

"Don't look at me," Gary continued. "I just drove all the way from Wisconsin today. My parents rent a cabin there every summer. I lay out on the boat while my father fishes." Gary acted like he was casting a line into the water, and I was a bass. "I think I got a good one," he said with a big laugh.

Gary was the most "out" out person I had ever met, so comfortable with himself that it made me instantly comfortable with myself.

We chatted and then I said we were headed to the bars.

"Oh," Gary said. "Bye."

We said our goodbyes, left and headed to the bar. I was being hit on by a "faux" Swedish guy who actually attended a local community college when Gary approached out of nowhere and busted the guy for pretending to be someone he wasn't.

"You have to be careful," Gary said. "Everyone can spot a newbie."

I told Gary my friend had left and that I didn't have a ride home. It was a trick that had worked many times for me already. When we got back to my bungalow, I put the moves on Gary, and he started to cry.

He had recently stopped drinking. He was not supposed to go to bars, much less be in a relationship with anyone until he had his sobriety under control. He was having job troubles.

I held Gary on my couch until he stopped crying.

"Why did you follow me somewhere you weren't supposed to be?" I finally asked.

"Had to follow my gut. I have great instincts."

Really? I thought.

I sent him on his way and went to bed, lamenting a wasted night.

The next day, Gary left a message for me. He was moving apartments. He gave me his address. I listened to the voice mail about a dozen times. He just sounded so…nice. So different from the guys I was meeting in bars.

On a whim, I drove over and helped. I met Gary's friends. We went on a proper date later that week. I was so nervous, I forgot my wallet. He thought I was a liar and, worse, broke. I left him sitting in the restaurant while I drove to an ATM to get some cash. He teared up when I returned.

"You're one of the good ones!" he said. "You came back! With money!"

He was funny, like my family and friends. He had a huge personality, like my mom and dad. He loved his family. And he was the most honest person I'd ever met.

After a few dates, Gary said he couldn't see me anymore. He said I was too newly out, I didn't know myself and I would end up hurting him. He could not harm his new-found sobriety.

I respected his decision but was devastated. I gave him time before calling him and telling him we had started something special, and one day he would realize that.

After a few months, he did.

"Your son has the biggest heart in the world," Gary says, looking directly at my dad. "He loves the two of us more than he loves himself. He is the best person I've ever known. I never felt safe until I met him. I never felt un-conditional love. He learned that from his family."

Gary is crying. My father's head is turned toward the window, and he seems to be scrutinizing the old oak.

"He learned that from his mother," my father finally says.

"But she married you. And you raised him. She didn't do it alone."

My dad looks at Gary. His bottom lip is quivering.

My father is the most sentimental-unsentimental man I've ever known, besides myself, emotions stuffed deep inside, a man handcuffed to time, pig-tied by geography, and gob-smacked by a son he lost and a son he never understood.

"Now it's your turn," Gary says. "Tell me a story."

I kick him again. My father's stories are too often just like the swift knock to the shins I gave Gary: painful, shocking, out-of-the-blue shiners.

Like the story my father once told Gary about his childhood. He and his friends used to wander the woods, crawl through storm sewers, race along the train tracks. One time, he found a litter of kittens in a pillowcase. They had been tossed out and left to die. One of the cats, my father said, had been born with two of everything: Two heads, two tails, too many paws and claws.

"Oh, my gosh," Gary had said. "Did you save it? What happened?"

"We killed it," my dad told him. "Put it out of its misery. Poor thing. We hated to see it suffer. What do you do with something like that—something so different that the only thing you know it will endure is pain and suffering?"

Gary grew emotional when he told me that story. Not just because of the horror of hearing kids kill something so innocent instead of trying to help it but because it summed up our lives in rural America.

What do you do with something like that—something so different that the only thing you know it will endure is pain and suffering?

The 1970s–1990s

My mother believed in equal parts medicine and miracle, and in my lifetime, I saw this combination work wonders more often than not. She was the go-to gal for locals who blistered their skin canoeing on the crick in the blazing summer sun or those who drunkenly tumbled down a hill while hunting, just as she was on-call for abandoned strays and abused animals.

I watched her perform her M&M ritual hundreds of times on neighbor and stray, both of whom shared similar traits in the Ozarks: hard lives, hard luck, often abandoned, often unloved. None of those lost souls had much money or hope, much less anyone in which to turn, save for my mom.

I grew up on a large swath of oak-knotted, sassafras-clotted, poison-ivy dotted woods in rural Missouri, and our land became a dumping ground for animals, often because folks knew that "woman in white"—which is how they referred to my mom in her starched white nurse's uniform—would do her damnedest to help those in need.

"I hear a cat," my mom would say while eating dinner, the patio door open, before setting off—still chewing her potato, now carrying a slice of bread—onto a leaf-strewn trail that led deep into the woods. And back she would come with a hurt kitten, or four.

My mother had a sixth sense for those in pain, those in need, and she would head out—day or night, barefoot, barely dressed—to assist the injured.

Over time, people got wind that my mom was a hybrid Florence Nightingale–Dr. Doolittle, and that our towering Arkansas stone house was a virtual land-bound ark.

In the Ozarks, the Rouse House became a sort of church for lost animal souls.

We had an endless parade of strays, and our garage became an animal infirmary: one of the stalls for cats, and the loft built above the garage near our back door for dogs.

There was the litter of burned hound dogs and the army of sickly feral cats that my mother saved: I remember how, with our local vet not on call, she choked back tears as she wrapped those hounds in cheesecloth, how she donned oven mitts and a donated catcher's mask to avoid the sharp claws and teeth to help those frightened, skinny, tick-riddled cats.

Needle in.

Needle out.

Head bowed.

My mom found good homes for those hounds, with us adopting one who was too injured to survive but did, for many years. And those feral cats never left our yard again: they would come close enough to eat, but hissed at anyone in the family except for my mom. She had saved their lives, and they would never forget. One by one when they were old enough, she took them all to get spayed and neutered, and they all lived long lives, especially the sickliest, Squeaky—named after the only noise it could make when it was little—who my mom adopted and brought inside. But Squeaky never forgot her feral ways: she would pounce on everyone in the house—as if they were surely going to attack her—save, of course, for my mom.

All of my pets growing up were rescues, and all had been found near death. There was Racer, my beagle; Charlie, the Shih-Tzu; Tricky Dick, the Chihuahua my grandparents adopted.

"You name them, Wade," my mother would tell me. "You're more clever than the lot down here. Lord knows we don't need another Spot or Whiskers in this world."

And glorious names those strays were given. My mom and I believed—after the lives they led—they needed to have royal, weighty names, like Brutus and Galileo. Or baseball heroes: Babe, Hank, Willie Mays or Ty.

But sometimes, like with a dim-witted Maine Coon we found, Maynard just seemed to fit.

"We got too damn many pets," my dad would yell when another stray would join the family. "This isn't a halfway house."

My mother would just stare at my father, hands on her hips, and say in her syrupy Ozarks drawl that was slow as refrigerated molasses, "Ted, you old goat-witch. We're not just saving these animals. They're saving us."

My father ended up dearly loving each and every pet. When they would pass, he would mourn, releasing more emotion than he ever showed for any human. We had a makeshift graveyard a ways into the woods, past the bramble, in a clearing, where the moon could shine through the oaks and "God could watch over them clearly," my mom said.

My dad would visit the graveyard a few times a year. Sometimes I would follow him and watch him talk to the makeshift crosses and their plots, which we outlined with stones in the shape of a heart. Sometimes, he'd catch me and yell, "Go home, boy!", and I'd scurry away to avoid upsetting him further.

A few nights a week when the weather was warm, my mom and I would walk in the woods with our strays, because nothing, I learned from my mom, bonded a family of strays more than a walk.

"And every family," my mom said many times, "is really a family of strays."

She would always ask my dad to walk with us, bond with us. He always declined.

My mother saved many lives. But it wasn't until later in life—on her final walk with my rescue dog, Marge, that I realized the meaning of my mother's words and actions.

"Why doesn't Dad ever come with us?" I asked her.

She stopped in the woods, the sunlight illuminating her face, but didn't turn around.

"No one's ever bonded with your father," she said. "Not even me. He won't let that happen because he's too afraid of being hurt. Only these animals he says he hates are capable of that because they don't pose a threat." She turned. "Imagine what it must be like for a father to have lost a son and be incapable of expressing that grief. He's just like a lot of these strays. They've been hurt so much in the past that the only way they know how to react to affection is to lash out for fear of being hurt all over again. Sometimes it takes a lifetime of love before a feral cat will let you pet it. Sometimes that never happens. Doesn't mean it doesn't want, need or deserve our love, the poor thing just doesn't know how to show it back."

October 2015

My grandma always said the most beautiful flowers were the weeds that grew in the ditch. Common little plants with gorgeous names: Queen Anne's lace. Goldenrod.

She would pick them and place them in her "purtiest" vase because, as she said, "They deserved a place of honor for growing up to be so beautiful despite all the circumstances set against them."

"Did I ever tell you the story of how I met your mother?" my dad asks.

We shake our heads no, although we've heard the story a hundred times, mostly from my mom.

The night my father rang the doorbell at my mother's apartment in Springfield, Missouri, for their first date, she answered it wearing a football helmet.

"Big game?" my dad joked.

"Bad dye job," she said. "My hair is white. Actually, it's green-white. Like infected pus."

Thankfully, neither her *M*A*S*H* humor, nor her hair, daunted my father-to-be.

"I have a strong stomach, and I'm a little color blind, so why don't you lose the helmet, Fran Tarkenton, and let's get a move-on," my father said, referencing the former Minnesota Vikings quarterback.

When my mother refused, my father simply ordered a pizza, and they had a picnic in the park across from her apartment.

For their second date, my mother cut off all of her badly damaged hair, so that only a tiny, fine amount remained, like you might find on a Barbie doll crammed in a box during a yard sale.

"It's just hair," my mother said, as a way to challenge my father.

He took her to a nice restaurant, to prove to her how much he liked her and how little he cared about what people thought.

"God has a great sense of humor," my mother told him that night, "and He loves to test us in the most peculiar ways."

My father had no idea.

And no matter how much he acted like he didn't care what people thought, he did immensely.

Long before Gary met my dad—when I would go to games with my best friends, or sit and watch a game with Gary's father—he would question why sports were such a bond for men.

"Because we're together," I said.

"But you're not sharing anything," he'd say. "You're not doing anything together. You're just sitting there on your butts, drinking beer, yelling for a team filled with players you'll never know."

"Oh, but we are. We're sharing everything without ever saying a word. We're sitting beside one another, pouring out our emotions for a team—for a group of guys we'll never meet—which is the only way we can do it."

"Do what?"

"Show our love for one another."

Spring 1998

Ironically, Gary met my father for the first time at a sporting event. I knew the introduction had to take place on neutral ground, and for my father that meant a sporting venue where he would feel most comfortable and in control. I considered a baseball game. It was spring, the daffodils were blooming, and I wanted my world—like the new season—to be filled with eternal hope again.

But the thought of being trapped in my own home with my father should things go south more quickly than a New Jersey snowbird was too much to consider.

So we settled on Hot Springs, Arkansas, a town known for its natural springs and mineral baths as well as the thoroughbred horse races at Oaklawn. My parents had come here for years to watch the horses and see the dogwoods bloom.

The scene at the racetrack was always part Kentucky Derby and part rodeo: wealthy young white women in colorful flowered hats the size of umbrellas and their elderly husbands in suits and ties sipping on 7 and 7s and daiquiris in their luxury boxes while country men and women in cowboy hats, dirty jeans and boots bet money they didn't have from the "infield," a crowded oval sitting in the middle of the track that provided only glimpses of the horses from ground level as they raced by.

My parents were seated in a luxury box near the finish line. Gary—despite my father's refusal to acknowledge he existed—actually got the box from one of his clients not only to impress my father but also to help soothe the sting of this first meeting.

I saw my parents as we rounded the corner. My mother, fittingly, was wearing a neon purple dress with a horse brooch the size of an actual horse, and horseshoe earrings. For some reason, however, she was sporting white tennis shoes and socks as if she might have to make a run for it at some point in the day. My father was holding a full beer in his left hand while scribbling notes with his right into the racing sheet perched on his lap.

As we made our way down to the box, I felt as if I might faint and fall down the steep narrow band of steps, a concussion a better option than this meeting. Gary put his hand on my back and said, "I knew I should've worn a hat!" I laughed. Like a bat, my mother turned at the sound of my voice. She looked neither happy nor sad, shocked nor relieved. She simply looked tired. I saw her whisper, "They're here," and my father turned only after killing half his beer.

"I'm Gary Edwards," Gary said. "It's nice to finally meet you in person."

"Ted Rouse!" my father shouted at the top of his lungs. "Damn glad to meet ya."

My dad slapped Gary hard on the back, making him stumble forward, bumping my dad's beer. This was not a good start to the day.

My mother embraced me with all her might.

My father turned without greeting me. No hug, no handshake, nothing. "Boy," he mumbled.

Gary tried to cover, as he usually does, by rambling. "It is so good to meet you both. I know this is awkward, but I've looked forward to this day since I met your son. He's an amazing person, and he loves you both very much."

My mother looked nervously at my father. He could not even look at us.

Gary continued undaunted. "Am I underdressed for the races? Should I go buy a bolo or perhaps a shirt that says, 'I Lost All My Money On Women and Horses… Not Necessarily In That Order'?"

My dad turned and stared at Gary with an open mouth. Less than a minute into this meeting, and Gary had already dumbfounded my father. My mother, picking up on the tension, thought she was nervously fingering her horse brooch but she was actually massaging her own boob. My dad chugged the rest of his beer before turning to Gary.

I held my breath.

"Have a seat," he said. "I gotcha some racing forms already."

Gary looked at me cluelessly, gently taking the racing form as if he'd been handed a newborn. I sat down and scanned the vista. It was a beautiful spring day; tulips were blooming around the track, and dogwoods had turned the Ouachita Mountains in the distance white. The horses—

solid muscle—were being trotted, the jockeys in their bright silks laughing with one another before their day began. No one was talking. We were suddenly the quietest ones at the track.

Out of nowhere, an elderly woman in a First Lady suit, gobs of diamonds and a red hat festooned with fresh flowers appeared.

"Y'all must shorely be the Rouse clan," she said in a syrupy Arkansas twang. My father was horrified, stunned that someone, anyone, on this of all days—the meeting of father and gay son's partner—knew him. We all continued staring at her in silence, no greeting exchanged, nothing resolved.

"I just love your hat!" Gary finally said. "And those flowers. It really is a work of art."

"Oh, my, ain't you a charmer?" she said. "I'm Mrs. Littlefield, and we race horses with the friends of yours who have this box here. They said to keep a lookout for y'all and say howdy, so I'm just bein' neighborly. It's so charmin' to meet y'all!"

She gave a polite wave and departed.

"Loved her hat," Gary said. "Now, that says, 'I've got money, and I don't care who knows.'"

My dad was again staring openmouthed at Gary, who's not big on silence. "So what do we do with this here racing form, Ted?" Gary asked. "See, I can do the racetrack talk."

"You study it, boy," my dad said. "Let me show ya."

I eavesdropped, trying not to be too conspicuous, as my dad explained how to study the racing form—times and finishes of past races, winning percentages of the jockeys and trainers, whether the horse was taking Lasix or wearing blinders. Gary was nodding, but not a word was sinking in. I knew he'd just pick the prettiest horses or the ones with the funniest names, or if a jockey was wearing his favorite colors. I didn't expect him to tell my father, but he did.

"Wanna know my secret, Ted?" Gary asked. "It's all in the gut. There's a horse in the first race called Leo's Gal. I'm a Cancer, so I get along with strong Leo women. My mom's a Leo, Geraldine's a Leo, so this horse is destined to win."

"Boy," my dad said, "that horse is a piece a' shit! She's outclassed here. Too small and too damn slow. She ain't won nothin' at this level. Why don'cha take a look at Pecan Pie? She's got a helluva pedigree."

"Oh, I have nut allergies," Gary said. "I can't bet on a horse that I'm allergic to."

This is not good, I thought.

I again felt dizzy and realized how smart my mother was for wearing tennis shoes. That was when I realized she was gone. My heart began to race, but when I turned, she was coming down the stairs with a tray of beers the size of fire hydrants and a soda for Gary.

I polished off a quarter of my beer and felt woozily better.

My dad placed twenty dollars on Pecan Pie—a huge bet for him—who finished seventh. Gary placed five dollars on Leo's Gal to show. The horse finished third with twenty to one odds.

The whole day, of course, ended up following this bizarre pattern. The favorites all lost, and the also-rans—with names like Cher's Delight, Mama's Boy and Sticky Buns—all did well, making Gary look like a gay Jimmy the Greek.

But somewhere during the course of this very stressful

day—perhaps between my father's fourth and fifth fire hydrant—he started to laugh with Gary, to call him "hon." To put his arm around him, just like he was a real person.

Over dinner at the town's old barbecue joint, my dad looked up at me when Gary went to the bathroom and spoke to me for the first time all day.

"He's a good person," my dad whispered. "I can tell lickety-split." He stopped. "I guess I shouldn't have expected anything else from you. Your mom always said you're a magnet for goodness."

His face was covered with barbecue sauce, and he was happily drunk but remarkably sober. He was looking at me square in the eye, another first today. It was then I saw he was crying. His tears were clearing paths through the sauce, and I wanted to cry, too. I looked over at my mom, who was gnawing a rib bone; there was no meat on it.

"I lost two years of my life without my only son in it," my dad said, "and I can never get that back."

He did not say he was sorry, and he did not ask for my forgiveness, but I could see his heart had been as broken as mine was.

Gary appeared and sat down at the table. "Ted, I think you could use a napkin," he said.

"Thanks, hon," my dad bellowed.

Summer 2010

One night at the cabin, my father and I got into a shouting match, supposedly over a Cardinals game. The Cards had blown a big, early lead, and my father wanted to stop watching. I, of course, wanted closure. I also just loved the sound of a summer baseball game in a cabin. It was soothing, nostalgic, and reminded me of my childhood with my grandparents at our old log cabin, my grampa constantly adjusting the transistor radio, Jack Buck's voice fading in and out. My father was raging at everything wrong with the team, but his rage was also directed largely at me. I was not coming to the cabin enough to help him out with all of his chores, and he wanted me to mow the lawn, wash the windows, hose away the spiderwebs and stain the deck.

"We can hire that out, Dad," I said. "I bet you know some handymen around here who could use some work."

"You lazy sum-bitch," my dad said. "You need to earn your keep."

I smiled. "I do earn my keep, Dad. But I only get a few days off a year. I came to spend time with you."

"You'll do as I say, boy."

My head spun. I'd had enough.

"Fuck you, you pathetic drunk."

He charged at me, but Gary stepped in, and my father stopped, like an old bull at his last fight.

I apologized, my father grunted and I went to bed early. Gary stayed with my father to calm him and monitor his drinking. I never allowed Gary to stay alone with my dad, as I didn't want my father's drinking to dredge up Gary's painful past with alcohol. But he had also been a sponsor to many alcoholics and helped a large number get sober.

"I know how to handle a drunk," Gary whispered to me. "Takes one to know one."

The deck over the water was positioned just below the guest bedroom upstairs. My windows were open to get some air, since it was about a hundred degrees upstairs. I heard my father and Gary talking. I stood on the mattress and put my ear to the screen.

My father was crying. Not just crying, but blubbering.

"I never knew what to do with him," my father said. "I still don't."

He quieted, and the rush of the water returned.

"It's like askin' me to land a plane or wrestle a bear," he continued. "I ain't got no manual."

"But you do," Gary said. "You're a father. Tell Wade you love him. Tell him you're proud of him. It's like he's been in the desert for years fighting to survive, and he just needs a little drink of water to keep going. Give it to him."

"I ain't got no manual for that neither." My dad hesitated. "Even the way he looks at me… He just wants things I can't give him."

"Like love? A hug? Acceptance? Those are easy things, Ted."

"Why did God give me a son like that? Todd was easy. Wade ain't."

"Maybe God wanted to bless you," Gary said. "Maybe He wanted to teach you things you needed to learn. Maybe He just wanted you to have the best son in the world because He knew you would need one right now."

My father began to weep anew.

"You still have one son who's alive, Ted," Gary finally said. "And he's right here with you. Don't bury him, too."

Someone across the river at the nearby campground screamed, a guttural yell that echoed down the water and along the muddy banks. I opened my mouth as wide as I could standing there in that window, and I let this lonesome stranger's sad, drunken release serve as mine.

7TH INNING STRETCH

"Let me root, root, root for the home team,
If they don't win, it's a shame..."

October 2015

The Cardinals put a man on base with a walk, but the Cubs easily retire the last two hitters.

The camera pans the crowd at Wrigley as the game goes to the seventh inning stretch, a moment of celebration in baseball and especially in Chicago. For decades before he died, famed Cubs announcer Harry Caray popularized the singing of "Take Me Out to the Ball Game." He would start with his trademark opening—"All right! Lemme hear ya! Ah-one! Ah-two! Ah-three! Take me out..."—and then hold out the microphone from his broadcast booth to capture the crowd around him singing.

Caray was a longtime Cards broadcaster before an infamous falling out with the team and its owner. There were many rumors about why Caray departed the Cardinals, but for many St. Louisans, his future loyalty to the Cubs only made the rivalry that much more fun and intense.

"Ol' Harry Caray," my dad says in remembrance. "Crazy sum bitch."

Takes one to know one, I think.

My mind clicks back to a seventh inning stretch with my father in St. Louis. I had arranged a surprise gift for my father, one I knew would impress him. I had Joe Buck—the famed sports broadcaster and son of Cards legend Jack Buck, who once broadcast alongside Harry Caray—autograph a copy of an interview I had done with him. Buck was an alumnus at a prestigious private school where I worked, and I interviewed him for the alumni magazine, which I edited. I had Buck sign a copy of the magazine for my father when it was published. I told him I wanted to give it to my dad at an afternoon Cardinals game. I told him how much my father loved the team. My father arrived in St. Louis for a visit. He hadn't come to see me, I knew, he had come to see the Cardinals. It was a beautiful warm afternoon, the beer was cold, and I'd gotten us seats from a friend who had season tickets just behind home plate.

It was the seventh inning stretch when I gave the gift to my dad. He was happily drunk. The Cards were winning. He had the best seats of his life. Ernie Hayes, the longtime organist at Busch Stadium, was playing. I had done good.

My dad opened the gift, looked at me and said, "He will never be the man his father was."

I was buzzed, too, but not happily so any longer.

I looked at my dad and said, "No, he won't, because he became his own man. And that's the hardest thing a son will ever do in his life. Not become a real man but become his own man."

I walked out of the game on my father. I still don't know how he made it back to my house, drunk and alone, using public transportation, late that night. My mother, who had gone shopping, didn't even bother to worry, much less look for him.

"Your father is out having drinks with strangers he met at the game who believe he's not only the life of the party but a helluva good guy," she said. "But he'll come back when he damn well wants to. Every baby needs his bed and his bottle."

I watch the seventh inning stretch in Chicago as the camera pans the crowd.

Young couples kiss. Some dance and drink beer. Others hug.

I smile, but my heart pangs. I missed all of this growing up, these simple adolescent acts of love, dating, dancing, finding yourself.

Becoming my own man.

My crushes in middle school, my secret crushes in high school, my longing in college went by without a passed note, a prom dance, a fraternity formal.

I was thirty-one when I decided I deserved to be loved and treated just like everyone else. It wasn't fair, and it never will be. And that sticks in my soul. The last chapter of my life may be a happy ending but the first part of my story wasn't just erased, it wasn't even lived.

My mother believed I found the perfect match in Gary because I spent my whole life searching not just for love but for the right person. I know she had the right intention when she attempted to romanticize my relationship, but it was spoken by someone who never had to worry about staring at a boy she liked too long, or been forced to ask a girl to a dance for which she had no feeling, or taught to learn that how she lived and loved was wrong, or to have had a Supreme Court decision determine if she could marry alter the very course of her life. It was spoken with great love but without ever having to watch every word you said and every move you made.

Without inventing a different version of yourself.

I listen to the Cubs crowd sing, and the soundtrack of my life fills my head.

Fall 1976

I had a beard long before I could even grow peach fuzz.

Her name was Lisa.

She was a perky, popular, pretty blonde (think Marcia Brady if you're over forty and Hannah Montana if you're under).

In my rural grade school, she intercepted a mood ring I had bought as a gift for my first crush, a boy with eyes the color of the public swimming pool.

"He was just joking. Wade's funny," Lisa explained to the kids in the cafeteria as they began to mock me, stealing the too-big ring and slipping it over her thumb. "See, it fits! Now, we're going steady."

My heart stopped that second, and a few things became crystal clear: I hadn't before realized that what I felt was wrong until I saw my crush cringe when I tried to give him the ring. I needed to lie about myself in order to survive. And the color of that mood ring quickly turned from dark blue (happy) to black (depression) on Lisa's finger.

I "dated" Lisa off and on for years: fall formals, homecoming dances. I was her fallback when she broke up with a boy and needed a shoulder; she was my beard when I needed to squelch rumors.

Lisa and I never talked about the fact I was gay. We couldn't really. We didn't even have a vocabulary for such a thing in the 1970s Ozarks, where the local men made the fellas from *Deliverance* look like the Jonas Brothers. I had no role models. I didn't even know what "gay" was. I just assumed Lisa knew I wanted a boyfriend as badly as she did.

To me, our relationship was similar to that of Bret Somers and Charles Nelson Reilly on my favorite show, *Match Game*: friends who understood the game each was playing.

I would learn, however, that our relationship was more serious to her: she loved my humor, my sensitivity and kindness.

She loved *me*.

And she would tell me that at a homecoming dance as we swayed to Journey's "Open Arms" on our gym's basketball court. I smelled of Polo. She smelled of Love's Baby Soft. The gym smelled of sweat.

"I love you," she whispered into my ear, brushing her cheek against my face, kissing my neck.

"I love you," I stammered, pushing her away. "But I don't *love* you."

The last song I heard filtering through the doors of the gym as I sprinted to my car was, appropriately enough, A Flock of Seagulls: "And I ran… I ran so far away…"

I wouldn't stop for decades.

When I returned to school that Monday, I discovered the

childhood mood ring that started our un-love affair taped to the front of my locker.

The stone was black.

And it stayed that way: I would blow on it, I would leave it on our stone patio in the sun, I would warm it in my hands, begging it to come back to life.

It remained black. Just like my love life.

After Lisa, I entered college and a downward spiral. I put on weight—consciously and unconsciously—in order to bury myself, feeling if I could make my body sexually unappealing to both men and women, I would render myself incapable of hurting anyone. I gained 120 pounds.

And yet all the things Lisa loved about me, other women did, too: My sensitivity. My kindness. My humor. So, I continued choosing beards rather than boyfriends, believing a life filled with false love was better than one filled with hate from family and friends, many of whom belittled gays, said they wouldn't accept anyone who was gay and believed that "my lifestyle" was a one-way ticket to hell.

Susan, a "little sister" in my fraternity, was my college beard. She was a brilliant artist and debater, and we would stay up late into the night fighting over everything from Reagan's policies to our favorite MTV VJ. I encouraged her to make her opinions known through art.

After stringing her along for years, our end came with my near-death at a fraternity fall formal when Susan lured me into a hayloft at a brother's farm to "seal the deal."

I smelled of Drakkar Noir. She smelled of Opium. The barn smelled of cow manure.

"I love you," she whispered into my ear, brushing her cheek against my face, kissing my neck.

The same words, spoken in the same quivering breath, that Lisa had spoken. This time, "Word Up" by Cameo was playing. This time, I couldn't run.

So, I did the only thing I could: I rolled myself off the edge of the hayloft and plummeted toward the ground. I was drunk. I was certain I was going to die. The last thing I remember seeing was Susan's face calling, "I love you!"

"I love you, too, but I don't *love* you," I thought before landing on a pile of hay. My back was black and blue for weeks, but my secret remained intact.

Next on the Beard List was Brandywine, a stripper I met attending a college friend's thirtieth birthday party. I bought her a beer; her gift to me was a private dance.

Brandywine attempted to ride me like a mechanical bull, to no avail. She finally forced one of her banana-shaped breasts into my mouth, thinking that might do the trick. I spit it out as a baby might a pacifier.

I complimented her instead: her stilettos, her human-hair wig. That's when I saw she had a wordy tattoo that read, "Forgiveness is giving up all hope of having had a better past."

"Anne Lamott?" I said, flabbergasted.

"Yes!" she screamed.

She looked into my eyes and said, "You're going to change my life," before adding, "All your friends are lookin'. Let's give 'em somethin' to talk about."

She French-kissed me so deeply, her chewing gum became mine.

"She likes you," my friends cajoled me. "You should ask her out."

I did, to continue my lie.

Wade dating a smart stripper. My reputation went through the roof.

Brandywine told me her real name was Alice. She was attending a community college and aspired to be anything that didn't require nudity.

Sans her stripper attire, Alice certainly looked, well, like an Alice.

I took her to a few parties. But when I didn't engage in sex after months, Alice saw through my act.

"Say it," she said.

"I'm gay," I said, bursting into tears. "My friends don't know, my family doesn't know, no one knows."

Alice held me. "Don't waste your life hatin' yourself, like I have."

I went to see her a few weeks later. I was depressed, lonely, still too scared to come out. Alice blew me a kiss while she twirled on a pole.

Then she took me behind a curtain and said, "I love you." She whispered into my ear, brushing her cheek against my face, kissing my neck. "You're the only man who's ever believed in me."

I smelled of Paco Rabanne. She smelled of whiskey and White Diamonds. The bar smelled of cheap perfume, cigarettes and vomit.

This time, "Cherry Pie" by Warrant was playing.

"I love you, but I don't *love* you," I said, running out of the strip club.

When I met Gary at a coffeehouse—in the days before coffee was cool and cell phones existed—it was a time when being gay in the Midwest meant you still remained largely in the closet. But there was no closet big enough for Gary, perhaps because there was no room left in it due to the circumference of his parachute pants. Still, my heart stopped the moment I met this tanned tornado of total transparency.

"You have the prettiest eyes I've ever seen," Gary said to me at one point.

"That's a terrible line," I said, looking around nervously to see if anyone knew me.

"It's not a line," he said. "They tell a story. And it hasn't always been an easy one."

For once in my life, I thought about what it would be like to kiss someone I really liked.

That happened a few weeks later.

"It's one of the sweetest things anyone has ever done for me," Gary said on the stoop of his new apartment after I'd helped him move. "I'm ready for our first official kiss now."

"Excuse me," I said, scanning the sidewalk for anyone I might know.

"You've been dying to kiss me all night so just do it already," he said. "And stop worrying what everyone thinks."

I leaned in, knowing this was the moment I'd waited for my whole life. And the wait was worth every minute.

"That was nice," Gary said. "You smell like home."

When I told Gary I loved him, I also told him about my beards. He told me to make amends, just as he had done in AA. "Do you know how much hurt you've caused over the years?"

I did. And I didn't. I'd only been focused on my own pain.

So, I sat down and made a list I titled "Wade's Beards." It included all the women I'd strung along, lied to, hurt in some deep and meaningful way. I located them and sent each an apology letter.

Susan asked how my back was and forgave me. She had forged a successful career as an artist.

Alice had finished school, moved, married, no longer stripped.

Though they said I had hurt them, they said I had blessed them, too, made them so much better than they might ever have become. A great weight lifted.

I never heard from them again. And, for a long time, I never heard from Lisa. And then one day, she called.

"My son is gay," she said. "I don't know what to do."

It had been nearly three decades since I'd heard her voice. I now lived far from the rural town where I'd grown up. I had written books and lectured around the country on coming out and equality. I'd been with my husband for over fifteen years.

"What if my husband leaves me?" she cried. "What if he won't understand? What if I have to choose my child or my spouse?"

The same questions my mother—and Gary's mother—had uttered when we came out.

I suddenly realized that while everything in the world had seemed to change, nothing really had. Everything eventually still came down to fear, love, acceptance. Everything came down to a moment of truth and bravery.

As we spoke, I thought of Lisa standing in that blue formal, alone, in the gym.

"Remember homecoming?" I asked her. "Your son never has to feel that way. And neither does any girl who might fall for him."

"I know," she said. "How did you find such courage?"

"You," I said. "You helped me learn to love myself. I'm just so sorry I hurt you along the way. You were collateral damage, and I can never forgive myself."

"I forgive you," she said.

Over the next few months, Gary and I counseled Lisa and her son, encouraged them, linked them to experts.

She called one spring day a few years ago, when the daffodils were blooming and the world smelled of possibility. "We're moving to a bigger city. My husband is all for it. My son is thrilled." She hesitated. "He can date, he can be himself. He can eventually find love without…" she hesitated again "…all the collateral damage. I've always loved you."

"I've always loved you, too," I said.

She paused, and then asked out of nowhere, "Do you still have that mood ring?"

I laughed. "Yes. I could never throw it away."

"Think you can find it?"

I ran to the basement of our knotty-pine cottage, holding my cell. It took a while, but I found the ring squirreled away in a little jewelry box that had been stuffed in a container filled with memorabilia. I had to move an old garden gnome to retrieve it. I placed the ring on my pinkie.

"What color is it?" Lisa asked, her voice filled with as much hope as the spring air.

I looked. My heart filled with emotion.

"Dark blue," I replied.

October 2015

The camera focuses on the color of the Cubs uniform, and I look at my dad as the bottom of the seventh begins.

Dark blue.

On the third pitch, Kyle Schwarber homers, and the Cubs are up 6-4. The crowd goes berserk.

"Turn it off! Now!"

Gary puts down the magazine he is reading and looks at my dad.

"It's just a game, Ted," Gary says. "Not life and death."

My eyes widen at his choice of words. I look at my husband. They weren't a mistake, I realize. He meant to say them.

My mother always said the best relationships were the ones where your partner not only brought out the best in you but made you want to become an even better person.

When my parents first visited us in St. Louis—long after Gary had moved in—my mom was stunned at the transformation of my bungalow, both inside and out. Gary had painted the walls and decorated. He had landscaped the front and back yards, turning them into miniature botanical gardens.

"You needed so much love," my mother said one morning as we sipped coffee on the back deck, watching Gary water the flower beds. "You needed so much nurturing."

She watched Gary weed and talk to his flowers.

"Your father mows the yard clean," she finally said. "Ever notice that? No plants, no flower beds, no borders, no bushes, no flowering trees, nothing. It's a clean shot from the house straight to the edge of the woods. It's hard for him to care for things. It's easier to just remove them from the world he sees." She grabbed my hand. "But that fits with how he sees the world. Nothing can intrude upon his version of reality. But you...*you* always saw the world full of beauty and possibility. You were ready to grow. You just needed to be nurtured and loved. Gary did that."

"You did that, too, Mom."

"Not in the same way. And you had the clarity and courage to recognize what you needed, and that's a gift, too. Too many of us seek ourselves in a relationship. 'I want somebody who thinks as I do, likes the same things as I do, wants the same things I do.' But you and Gary want only to bring out the best in one another, plant dreams in one another and then work to make them grow."

We were making breakfast later that morning when my mom noticed the Valentine hanging on the refrigerator that I had made for Gary when we first met. It was a voucher in the shape of a heart, an IOU that stated, "I Promise to Love You for the Rest of My Life. You May Collect Daily!"

"Most people see their heart as a childish Valentine's

drawing, but it's actually a fist," my mom said. "You want someone that makes it pump faster, that makes it stronger every day."

The sound of the game knocks me into the present.

My mother was right. And wrong. I've actually come to believe that love takes on many different shapes or forms to each of us.

I think of what my father said to me so long ago.

"He will never be the man his father was."

Isn't that a good thing? Isn't that what fathers—what all parents—strive for? That their children will not be replicas of themselves but their own unique selves?

The Cards strike out the next two Cubs batters. I grab my phone and look up a statistic.

In the over 150 years of Major League Baseball history, and over 218,400 games played, there have been twenty-three official perfect games by the current definition.

No pitcher has ever thrown more than one.

You would think over that length of time, it would've happened, right?

But think of how hard it is not only to throw the perfect pitch time after time but also to throw the *right* pitch time after time. The chances are that, eventually, a pitcher will make a mistake: The fastball isn't on the corner but right down the middle of the plate. The curve doesn't curve. The sinker doesn't sink.

The optimist in me truly believed that a new day would bring a new chance for a perfect game. But it's difficult to navigate life in this way, feeling as if you're running across quicksand, praying every step is the right one and hoping against hope you won't go under by making a mistake.

I consider most relationships with our parents to be the equivalent of a perfect game. I know of some friends who have had seemingly ideal relationships with their parents. But when you ask, or dig deeper, you discover the truth. It's nearly impossible to have a perfect parent-child relationship.

Twenty-three of 218,400 games comes out to be a percentage of 0.000105311355311.

In other words, it's a damn near impossibility.

And yet every pitcher who walks out onto that mound every single game is striving to pitch a perfect game, just like every dad who holds his son for the very first time vows to be the perfect father. He will not be like his dad. He will make history.

What is a good man?

What is a bad man?

What is a real man?

What, simply, is a man?

Maybe it's owning up to your weaknesses, like knowing you can't hit a curveball, or that you'll never be fleet of foot, or that you can never drink again. Maybe it's letting go of everything and just learning to be. Maybe it's being a better person than you ever imagined. Or maybe it's just trying to be a decent one.

I don't know. I don't think I'll ever know.

But I do know love. All its beauty and horror, all its tricks and wonder.

I know because I waited my entire life to find it. I searched for it, like I used to do diamonds when my parents would take me to Arkansas gem fields, and I would dig in the dirt all day long, as though my life depended on it.

I lost a brother, a mother, nearly my entire family.

Yet here I sit watching a game with my father and my husband.

And I know love is not shaped like a heart.

We've had it wrong all these years.

It's shaped like a baseball.

Love may seem as round and as easy to toss about from one person to the next, just like an infielder warming up before a game. But it isn't. Love comes right at you, pitch after pitch, inning after inning, game after game, season after season: sometimes it's a fastball, sometimes it's disguised as a knuckler, but most often love is a curve. You don't know where it's going.

Sometimes you'll miss it, badly. Sometimes you'll foul it off.

But sometimes you end up getting a mighty swing at it.

And if you make contact, you're not lucky. You're damn good.

Because you never took your eye off it, from beginning to end.

8TH INNING

"The Rivalry"

October 2015

The Cardinals go one-two-three lickety-split against the Cubs in the top of the eighth, striking out twice and looking overpowered by pitcher Pedro Strop.

"Hand me the remote," my father says.

I hesitate.

"Game's not over, Dad."

"My house! My rules!" he yells. "I ain't dead yet, boy. Hand me the remote!"

Gary is gone. It's just the two of us again. I grab the remote off the coffee table and hand it to him. I hold my breath.

He hits a button, and the channel changes to Fox News.

"No way!" I yell. "No way I'm watching this."

My dad glares at me.

Although we are a year out from the 2016 presidential election between Hilary Clinton and Donald Trump—and Trump is a decided dark horse and far from most people's minds that he would be the official Republican nominee—Gary and I have already predicted to friends that Clinton will lose to Trump. In fact, we are one hundred percent certain.

How do we know?

The past informs me.

When Trump formally announced his candidacy earlier this summer, and we would drive to visit my father, the landscape in rural America was clear: Gary and I passed hundreds and hundreds of Trump signs as well as hundreds and hundreds of anti-Hilary signs.

Trump, I knew, was already tapping into something others did not see, but that I did clearly: fear. The world was changing, quickly—from technology to a new economy—and a huge number of people felt as if they'd been forgotten and left behind. America was becoming more diverse. And this was not the America many knew any longer.

Including my father.

But my dad wanted it back. The past. Everything. Exactly the way it was.

"That sum-bitch says what's on his mind," my father says of Trump. "America needs to be great again."

"That sum-bitch is a monster," I say.

My father glares at me.

If you were to unleash a scroll listing the many things that have divided me and my father, politics would sit at the top of that list. In bold and all caps.

We were as red and blue as the Cards and Cubbies, just as big rivals when it came to politics.

"Let me ask you a question," I say. "Do you think he's a good person?"

"You don't have to be a good person to be a good politician," he says. "You don't have to be a good person to get shit done."

"Should you be a good person then?"

My father glares at me. He despises it when I turn the tables on him, make an issue real so he actually has to think and consider it.

"I can't wait to vote for Trump," my father says, looking me right in the eye.

He is goading me, just like Trump does others. I despise bullies. I hate little men with big mouths. I grew up with faux bravado masquerading as strength.

"You'll be dead and in the ground before this election," I finally say.

My father smiles.

He got just what he wanted. He turned my question around on me.

And I failed the test.

March 1965

I was born in 1965, the unlikely product of an ultra-conservative father and an independent-thinking mother. If Dick Cheney had fathered a child with Cher, I would be the result.

My birth came in the midst of a cultural shift in America, one that redefined my mom and unnerved my dad. My mother, a heretofore "good, conservative, Christian gal," according to my father, had not only voted for JFK but volunteered for his campaign, heresy to my Ozarks father, who loved Richard Nixon. My mother became a political pariah in southern rural Missouri, where your cultural options aren't really buffet style as much as they are prix fixe: Baptist or Southern Baptist; fried chicken or fried gizzards; sweet tea or sun tea; Republican or Republican.

The only way for my father to deal with my mother was to dismiss her beliefs on the basis of naiveté and feminine emotions. My dad believed my mom had been "starstruck" by JFK's good looks, much like she had swooned over Elvis, and that her "southern Southern parts" had overwhelmed her brain. My mom actually moved out of the house for a short time, but eventually returned, steadfast in her Democratic devotion to JFK.

When he was elected president, my mother said she had never felt prouder. When he was assassinated, my mother said she had never felt more adrift.

LBJ took office and helped continue JFK's agenda, ushering in a new era. All of this became a watershed moment in my parents' marriage: Could it survive politics? In an effort to make their union work, they decided—like so many couples in stressful times—to have a child, thinking perhaps a screaming infant would be the balm they required.

LBJ's Great Society program—civil rights, aid to education, attack on disease, Medicare, Medicaid, urban renewal, beautification, conservation, development of depressed regions, a wide-scale fight against poverty, control and prevention of crime, and removal of obstacles to the right to vote—became his agenda for Congress in January of 1965.

I was born in March. My mother called me the "Great Society baby" and my father only partially joked that I had a 50-50 chance of turning out okay.

The story goes that when my father held me in his arms for the first time, moments after I was born, he looked at my mother and said, "This boy's too pretty to be a Republican."

Yes, I was destined to become a liberal and a scourge to my father's every hope and belief. We would become a political Laurel and Hardy, Abbott and Costello.

Even in the dark days of dementia, when my father could

not remember where or who he was, he never forgot he was a Republican.

And I never forgot I was a Democrat.

1977

In middle school, my social studies teacher had the wonderfully creative idea that the class form its own new states and governments. This was in the year following the bicentennial, when America was still feeling decidedly united. The goal was to familiarize students with government and the duties of citizens within their government. Our class was divided into halves and tasked with electing officers, and creating branches of government, rules of law and a constitution. I was elected president of my state, which we called "Tronto: The Land of Sunshine."

I remember that my rule of law was quite simple: kindness.

"When creating laws," I remember essentially saying, "we must always ask ourselves, 'Is this good for all? Are we making the world a better place?'"

Our country's name, like my governing philosophy, was optimistically sunny. I ran into problems when I had to send our rules back to the citizens to be ratified.

"What about me?" was always the number one question.

I had my grandma, the seamstress, make a beautiful flag, with a giant sunshine peeking from the corner.

The local newspaper came out and took pictures of the president, senators and state reps. When the article appeared in the paper, my mother cut it out and hung it on the refrigerator, like most mothers did at that time. Over dinner, my father asked how the new state I was helping to create would be different.

I reiterated my philosophy.

My father considered this for a moment, pausing to lift his can of beer to his mouth, and then laughed very hard. He pointed his fork at me and said, "Well then, boy, your little experiment's gonna fail, because you can't make everyone happy. A country can't be based on bein' nice to everyone."

I stood, put my hand over my heart and recited the Pledge of Allegiance, emphasizing its final words: "...with liberty and justice for *all*."

"Isn't that why America was founded?" I asked.

"You sound like a damn Democrat," my dad said.

He stood and left the table.

The next day, my country's flag was stolen. My teacher found it stuffed in the corner of the coat rack behind our little jackets.

November 2012

"You know we're just gonna cancel each other out, right?"

It was roughly three years after my mother's death, one after my nightmare year. My father was sitting sideways in the passenger seat, his head against the window. He straightened, looked at me for a few beats and smiled mischievously.

"Always will." Beat. "Unless I outlive you."

I laughed, and my father tilted back against the window again, the sun illuminating his shrinking presence, the unkind gift of a long life. His memory was shrinking, too, the unkind gift of dementia. But today—Election Day, of course—his logistical, sharp-as-a-tack chemical engineering mind was intact.

"I'd hoped you'd have one of your off days and vote Democratic," I said.

"You'll never get that lucky. Straight Republican ticket," he said. "All I've ever voted."

"Never a Democrat?" I asked. "Even one? Ever?"

His laugh was dismissive. He doesn't find the humor in my question.

"NEVER!" he said proudly.

It was November, and most of the Ozarks trees were bare, save for the oaks, whose leaves clung stubbornly, just like my dad.

My father had experienced a bad few weeks, and I was home to see him, convince him to make more changes in his life, which I knew was as futile as asking him to mark a box for Obama, which I had already done.

I pulled up to the little town voting center, and he excitedly got out of the car and began to riffle through his wallet for his ID.

"Need any help?" I asked.

"NEVER!" he said proudly.

As he started to close the door, I asked—because I *had* to: "Dad, did you learn anything from me after all our political battles?"

He stooped down and peered back into the car. "It's only politics, boy. Nothin' personal."

He slammed the door, and I watched his little body in his little sneakers and little blue sweatsuit totter off to vote.

The man astounded me, and he knew it.

Because it had always been personal.

Rewind to Christmas four years earlier. My mother was dying. I had been taking her back and forth to chemo treatments. She called it one of her Christmas gifts, my companionship during chemo. Friends had taken her off and on, but I traveled back and forth from Michigan to help.

My father usually wasn't even around when we headed off for the morning.

I focused my attention on one of the stained-glass windows the oncology ward used to brighten the sterile space. It was of a dove with an olive branch flying over a rainbow. The window was ringed with sparkling holiday lights, and a little side table held a twinkling tree, both cords simply left to hang, joining the hundreds of other cords snaking to monitors and machines.

I thought of Gary, back cleaning my parents' house, who would have a conniption trying to hide all these cords.

I wondered if my mother would be around for other holidays—Valentine's, Mother's Day, Easter, Fourth of July—if we would get a chance to dye eggs, shower her with gifts, shoot off bottle rockets and make homemade ice cream. I stared at the tree: if I looked at my mother right now, I would start crying and possibly never stop. I did not want her to sense my fear, my terror, my pain, although I'm sure it was written all over my face.

I just wanted this to be a perfect Christmas, one free of drama, since it could be our last all together. But that was a lot to ask of my family. Obama's election had divided our family. My father was furious at my mother for not only voting for him but also publicly supporting him, as she did JFK and Carter, in the decidedly red area where they were born and raised.

When we finished, we returned home. I hydrated my mother and put her down for a nap in front of the fire and Christmas tree.

My father appeared, walked past her and said, "Guess I can't turn on the TV quite yet, huh?"

When my mom woke, Gary was waiting with a Christmas present.

"Oh, we can't open them until tomorrow," she said.

My family had a tradition that gifts not be opened until Christmas morning.

"I want you to open it now," he said, looking toward the stairway. "Just us."

My mom scooched up a bit on the couch, her face in pain, and Gary handed her the pretty package wrapped in vintage-looking paper and a velvet bow.

"Help me," my mom said to him.

Gary helped her unwrap the gift. She pulled a T-shirt from a raft of glittery tissue paper.

It was an Obama T-shirt that said Hope.

My mother teared up. "Thank you," she said. "I will wear this to chemo every day, as a symbol of hope for others to see."

I imagined my mom sporting a T-shirt with Obama's image on it to chemo in rural America. I could not imagine the looks—much less comments—she might receive. But my mother had always been stronger than anger, bigger than hate. My mom voted, as the shirt stated, for hope. My mom wanted a change in the world before she died. She wanted change for small towns and big cities, those in poverty and those who were sick. She wanted a youthful voice who embraced a changing America. My mom was tired of seeing Black families turned away at hospitals and sick of the racial hatred she heard spewed every day.

My mother didn't want to die without voting for Obama. One of her last wishes was to live long enough not only to vote for the first African American candidate to run for president but, hopefully, see him inaugurated. I actually think that gave her strength to continue.

"Can you imagine?" she had said. "The kind of message that signals to America. We can do better. We will do better. We are a better world."

"Put on the shirt," Gary said.

"Oh, no, I won't do that."

"Why?" he asked.

"We won. There's no reason to rub your father's nose in it. Wasn't that Obama's message? Hope. Unity. Ted may not have voted for him, but that doesn't mean we have to be mean."

"Mom, he has a gay son. He has a wife battling cancer. We are still fighting for our rights. The world is changing. Why can't he see that?"

"We all have mirrors, honey," my mom said. "But sometimes we don't see what's really being reflected back because we can only see an image from the past."

October 2015

The Cubs put two men on in the bottom of the eighth. There is only one out. My father is raging, furious at me, the Cards, the world.

He is dying and still at war with the world.

I feel like jumping up and running away.

Yet again.

The colors of the teams' uniforms are beyond ironic: red vs. blue.

Yet again.

The sun glints off something outside and sends a glaring light into the living room, which glows an eerie red. My father's eyes skew.

"Still got that nice red ride, huh?" my dad asks after a while.

"I do," I say. "Gotta have a red car once in your life, right?"

"I wish, boy," he says, before turning his bloated body toward me. "Too late to go for a ride, huh?"

He laughs, but it's a hollow one.

"Time shore goes fast, don't it, boy?" he asks. "That car a'yore's got some get up and go?"

"V-8. You remember?" I ask. "Don't you?"

He shakes his head no.

My father had a strict nightly routine when I was growing up: he would get home from work, pop a beer, read the financial section of the paper, curse at the news and then watch his favorite TV shows.

Among my father's favorites was a mystery called *Hart to Hart*. It starred Robert Wagner and Stefanie Powers as a rich, married, jet-setting couple who always seemed to be stumbling into murders and solving them. My father loved "whodunits," as he called them, but *Hart to Hart* also indulged his passion for cars.

The Harts tooled around SoCal in expensive convertibles, including a yellow Mercedes.

"Now, that's a beautiful car," my dad would say, his eyes wide with admiration as he downed a beer. "V-8, top down, hair in the wind…" Then he would sigh and say, "Some day. Some day."

That day never came. He just couldn't pull the trigger. Instead he drove a rusting white pickup truck with holes in the floorboard.

After my mother died, I was visiting my father—who was falling deeper into the throes of dementia—and as I was flicking through the channels, I came upon *Hart to Hart*. As a convertible raced down the highway in the opening credits, he smiled.

"I should have bought that car," my dad said, his eyes clear, his voice strong. "And now it's too late."

Later that year, when it came time to trade in our old car for a newer one, Gary texted me a photo of a red Thunderbird convertible—a fiftieth anniversary collector's edition. It was not what we had planned to buy.

Want it? Gary texted.

I thought of my dad, my childhood, *Hart to Hart*.

Yes, I wrote without hesitation.

I drove the convertible ten hours to see my father, and I will never forget his reaction when we wheeled him out to see it. His cheeks quivered.

Somehow, we got him into that car, and I drove him around his hometown—top down, gunning the V-8—the wisps of his hair flipping in the wind. A huge smile was plastered on his face. He was a kid again, free, living in the moment.

I drove him to his favorite spots, as he used to do me and Todd as kids on his weekend drives, and I tried to see the world through his eyes that day.

We were all products of our environment. My dad's world had not changed. I'm not saying that's a bad thing. Ask him what the most important attribute in life or politics is, and he will likely say, "Loyalty."

But in the time I left my Ozarks hometown, I have lived in cities across America. I have traveled to many places around the world. I have interviewed politicians and celebrities, and mothers of children in the inner city who have been killed. I am privileged, I know, but those dynamic environments changed my perspective. You see the world as a whole, not as a divided piece, isolated. You build empathy for others, not just yourself.

On the drive, I took my dad back to our cabin and down to see our old beloved swimming hole the locals called Straight Up Rock. Straight Up Rock rose straight up from the water and reached to heaven—the sun blinding you when you'd try to look at its highest point, and I nearly passed out the first time I climbed up and jumped. My dad was standing on the beach, yelling for me to do it.

"You ain't scared a' nothin' in this world, boy! You got it!"

That memory echoed in my mind: his methods may have occasionally bordered on insanity if not cruelty, but my dad was the one who taught me to jump, to not be scared, to believe in myself, that I could do it. And that made me speak my mind. That made me who I am. Too many in the world, however, don't have an advocate, much less a father who stuck around.

On the way back, my dad and I crossed the bridge where my brother was killed. Over time, it had been widened, from one lane to two.

"Smell them wildflowers?" my dad said in the convertible, sniffing the air like a happy dog. "Your grandma used to pick a bushelful there."

I used to go with my grandma to pick those pretty wildflowers so she could lay them at the place where her grandson died.

Perspective. Environment.

After that visit as I drove home, my father's image—and memories—filled my mind. And as the wind whipped my hair, I realized that life—like money—is often too short but that sometimes you have to put the top down and just enjoy the ride.

"Never pegged you for a red car man," my dad says.

"What is it they call red convertibles?" I ask him. "Pull-me-over red?"

He chortles. "Republican red."

I think of how quickly that convertible could speed me away from this place, to Chicago or St. Louis, only four and a half hours from here, but a world away.

St. Louis is, at heart, a big city that feels like a small town. You can go downtown or to a professional sporting event and be surrounded by fifty thousand people, or you can slip into one of the city's historic or suburban neighborhoods and feel like you're in a resort town.

One of the things I loved most about living in St. Louis and Chicago was the combination of diversity and invisibility both cities provided. No one stared at you for being different. You could slide into a booth at a coffee shop and sit for hours without anyone recognizing you.

In rural America, I often felt like I wore a target on my back.

I once tried to explain the way I felt to my father so he could understand. It was the midst of the Bush–Cheney years, in which states were essentially making marriage between two men unconstitutional. I felt adrift and isolated. I felt despised in my own country. I refused to go to church any longer. I tried, as I had done a million times, to try to see the world from a different, broader point of view. I said that his isolation from the changing world and being surrounded by people who often looked and thought like him had cultivated his way of thinking.

"Then don't get married," he told me.

"It's a right, Dad. I deserve the same rights as you."

"No, you don't."

"Why?"

"Because it ain't ever been that way."

"But that doesn't make it right. It just means the rules were made by people who only saw the world from their own point of view. I mean, women couldn't vote at one time. Interracial marriage was not allowed. Was that right?"

"You and your land of sunshine," he said. "Just like that fake state you created as a kid."

"Isn't that what we should strive for, though?"

"Ain't ever gonna happen."

"Doesn't mean you stop trying."

My father screams at the game, knocking me from that memory and into another.

I think of my first "liberal" friend from college, whose father was a judge and former state representative. It was the era of Ronald Reagan, and my friend was a lone liberal in the sea of college Republicans. He did not always agree with his very outspoken father, but he was compassionate, intelligent and ahead of his time.

"The very meaning of college is to be challenged," he told me. "Our thoughts and beliefs. We are surrounded by people of every background, race and religion, and their view of the world should change ours. Our parents should not raise us to be clones. And we only begin to change when we see the world through others' eyes."

That happened to me in college and graduate school.

My father accidentally hits the remote, and Fox News blares.

Growing up, the evening news was my father's therapy session. He would drink a beer and rage at the TV while my mom cooked dinner and my brother and I did homework. Journalists were the enemy of the people.

"Why do they have to stick their noses where they shouldn't?" he would ask no one. "They should do stories on things that take people's minds off the problems in the world."

To my father, journalists were not supporting democracy, nor did freedom of the press have anything to do with democracy; they were muckrakers, stirrers of trouble, agitators. My father didn't consider Woodward and Bernstein to be American heroes; he considered them traitors. They brought down *his* president for doing something he felt was perfectly fine—something every political candidate did— and he believes that to this very day.

It was the ultimate irony, I would later realize, because my father preferred to sweep everything under the rug. He preferred people see him and his family as the image he created and projected, not the reality of what existed.

I did not major in journalism to spite my father. I considered it a calling. Writing was a way I made sense of the world; journalism was a way I could be a voice for injustice in the world, much of which I had been on the receiving end all my life growing up as a smart gay kid in rural America.

Northwestern, especially, changed my life. And my perspective.

I was not only surrounded by students that were as smart or smarter than I was; I was surrounded by people of all ages, races, income levels and worldviews. Everything I wrote or said was challenged.

Moreover, I was taught what it means to be a journalist. Part of our initial semester was spent working "a beat," and our classroom was our newsroom. We were expected to file stories on time—banging them out on old typewriters, which meant deadlines were even more daunting, editing was done as we wrote, and mistakes had to be minimized. Every source I interviewed was turned in, every note and tape recording, and I was often told I didn't get enough points of view or talk to enough people. Every headline we wrote had to be better, more concise, more accurate. I covered Cabrini Green, Chicago's infamous housing project, and wrote stories about murder trials, horrific crimes against children living in poverty. Many nights, I would return to my studio apartment and scream while I was in the shower. By my last semester, my class was publishing a magazine, created, written, designed and edited by us. Our final grade? Sell that magazine to a mainstream publisher. We did.

I was front and center when news changed, and Fox came to be.

In 1987, the year I graduated college and started Northwestern, the FCC's fairness doctrine was removed. The fairness doctrine, introduced in 1949 when my father was a boy, was a policy that required the holders of broadcast licenses to present controversial issues of public importance and to do so in a manner that was—in the FCC's view—honest, equitable and balanced.

The fairness doctrine had two basic elements: it required broadcasters to devote some of their airtime to discussing controversial matters of public interest, and to air *contrasting* views regarding those matters. Stations were given wide latitude as to how to provide contrasting views: it could be done through news segments, public affairs shows or editorials. The doctrine did not require equal time for opposing views but required that contrasting viewpoints be presented. I consider the demise of this FCC rule to be a contributing factor for the rising level of party polarization in the United States as the main agenda for the doctrine was to ensure that viewers were exposed to a diversity of viewpoints.

When I started as a reporter, I once tried to explain to my father that even when writing a story about a traffic accident, I talked to multiple sources and tried to see it from every side.

Moreover, I took a headline-writing class that was devoted to accuracy; headlines were intended to be as newsworthy and accurate as the story itself, a thing of the past in these clickbait times.

While Fox became a legitimate news source for millions of Americans, for me it represented just how fragile a free and fair press can be, and that we should never take that for granted.

There is a story showing a distorted image of Hilary Clinton.

I grab the remote and change the channel back just in time to see the Cardinals get out of a bases-loaded jam.

"Well, I'll be damned," my father says. "Who woulda thunk?"

This is his attempt at momentary reconciliation.

"It's called hope, Dad," I say. "Nice way to look at the world, isn't it?"

He grunts, but then says, "You've always been a fella of conviction. Politics. Life. And you can't ask more than that out of a man now, can ya?"

I stare at him, openmouthed. I'm about to say something that might finally end this grudge match, even the score once and for all, but he seems to know that, so he wags a finger at me and grunts again.

"But there's right and wrong. And ya always been on the wrong side a' things, boy."

"Do you think Trump is a good person?" I ask once more.

"You don't have to be a good person to be a good politician," he repeats. "You don't have to be a good person to get shit done."

"Should you be a good person then?"

"Politics and life are two very different things," he says.

"You're right," I say. "But shouldn't we try for that?"

I stand suddenly, remembering, wondering if in all the carefully marked boxes and junk hoarded in his garage if…

I return with a surprise.

"Remember this?"

He shakes his head.

I hold up a thin, tattered piece of fabric.

"What the hell?" he asks.

"Tronto: The Land of Sunshine," I say. "The government I formed as a kid."

It takes him a while, but a light pops on like a gas flame in his faded blue eyes.

"I wanted my state to be all about kindness." I look at him. "What would happen if the two of us formed our government like I did in school?"

"We'd kill each other."

"Would we balance each other out?"

"We'd cancel each other out."

"Do you think we could find some common ground, though? Just a little? Enough to get stuff done for the good of not only both of us, but everyone?"

"What do you think?"

"I think we could," I say. "I think we've done that our whole lives, don't you? Tried to seek common ground, even though it may not have seemed that way. The world may be divided, and we may never see eye to eye on politics, but we're still here, in the same house, still talking, still listening, still wanting a better outcome for the future. Maybe that's a victory for both sides."

"Then why ain't we running the whole damn country?" He laughs before looking at the TV. "But that ain't happenin', is it? In politics or in homes? Folks ain't talkin'."

"Nope." I shake my head.

"Damn shame, ain't it?"

"Damn shame," I say.

I take the flag and drape it over my dad's back. He looks

at me and shakes his head, but then pulls the flag onto his lap and smooths it lovingly.

As if on cue, sunshine illuminates his body.

And the game goes into its final inning.

9TH INNING

"Game Over"

October 2015

Sometimes a game—and a season—ends with a whimper.

So it is with the Cardinals.

There is a tiny spark of hope in the top of the ninth, but it's not even an ember really. Matt Carpenter singles with two outs.

And yet my heart remains in my throat. I still believe the next batter, Stephen Piscotty, will launch a ball onto Waveland or Sheffield, and the Cardinals will pull out a miracle once again.

My father snores, and I choose not to wake him unless that miracle occurs.

Above his head, over the door, is a plaque that reads: "Forgive us our trespasses, as we forgive those who trespass against us."

Watching any sport, especially baseball, requires great faith. You have no control over the players on the field, or the outcome, but you certainly feel as though you do.

This must be how God feels, I've always thought.

My mother was a person of incredible skill *and* incredible faith. When my brother died, my mother left the church, as she felt our family was being used to raise money for it out of fear. My brother became a fundraising device.

Church didn't end, however: my mother became our family's minister, holding her own church services for me under the old oak on the Arkansas stone patio outside our house. The only parishioners were us, along with a group of occasional and curious squirrels, deer and chipmunks.

I remember her first sermon well: It was about faith, not religion. It was about hope, not fear. It was about acceptance and courage. It was about living honestly versus pretending to live. It was not the service of a preacher, practiced to perfection, shouted, fear dripping from the stained-glass windows. Her service was as uneven as the stone patio. But it was human, real, personal and heartfelt. My mother meant every word she said.

I even remember one of the verses she read, from *James* 2:14–26 ESV. It is still underlined in the Bible my mother left for me after she died.

What good is it, my brothers, if someone says he has faith but does not have works? Can that faith save him? If a brother or sister is poorly clothed and lacking in daily food, and one of you says to them, "Go in peace, be warmed and filled," without giving them the things needed for the body, what good is that? So also faith by itself, if it does not have works, is dead. But someone will say, "You have faith and I have works." Show

me your faith apart from your works, and I will show
you my faith by my works.

Over the years, my mother became a devout student of
world religion, and many of her services focused on Islam,
Hinduism, Buddhism and Judaism along with Christian-
ity. Many focused on kindness and being a good person.
Most focused on forgiveness. It was a lesson she seemed to
know I would need embedded deep inside me.

After a while, our back patio began to draw a congre-
gation of its own. At first, some of my mom's more open-
minded nursing friends joined us, and then a couple of
Catholics and Episcopalians who didn't have churches close
by. Finally, it was some townsfolk who had been cast out
by society: women my mom had helped, who knew that
their lots in life had been set by the men—fathers, husbands,
boyfriends, bosses—who had demeaned and abused them.

My mom sought a clearer understanding of not only why
man believed but why he hated.

It came down to organized religion.

Religion, *not* faith.

Not all took kindly to my mother's teachings, however.

We were shopping at the local grocery one afternoon
when a woman walked up and threw milk on my mother,
before squatting and taking a shit on the floor in front of
her.

"This is what God and I think of you!" she screamed.

I remember shaking so hard I could barely stand. My
mother offered to help clean up the mess.

Show me your acts.

I am a person of faith. I am often chided for that by my "intellectual" friends, ones who need an explanation for everything or can't find solid evidence that God exists.

"God is all around you," I tell them. "Life is just too intricate, too hard, too beautiful to be happenstance."

"But how do you know?" they push.

Some things you don't know. You believe.

Like if you're going to get a fastball or an off-speed pitch. If you're going to make a leaping catch, or the ball's going to sneak over the fence.

But some things you do.

Life—like the game—isn't just happenstance. You make decisions, inning by inning, that decide the outcome.

And I want to make the right ones.

That is faith to me. That my decisions, deeds and actions over the long haul matter. Not just to me, but to others. And God is Tony La Russa, watching, calculating, deciding if you'll make the starting lineup for the next game.

Am I silly to have such faith?

Perhaps.

Many friends say it's just my way of playing the odds. Just in case.

But they're wrong.

I *must* have faith. What other purpose is there for believing something incredible could happen tomorrow? That the next inning will be different?

My soul is a stained-glass window dropped from the heavens and then shoved back inside me, shards and all. They pierce me. And I would have it no other way. For it makes me feel EVERYTHING—all the good, bad, dark, light, joy, pain—and I want to feel that. I *have* to feel that.

I watch my father sleep.

I have to believe that my family will be waiting if I do. My brother will punch me in the shoulder. My mom will not let go of me for days, telling me stories for hours at a time—no commas or periods in any of them—about folks I need to meet and how much she's missed me. And my dad—after yelling, "Land the plane, Geraldine!" at my mom because her stories won't end—will pat some fluffy cloud on a beautiful summer day overlooking Busch Stadium, and I'll take a seat beside him and watch the Cards play a game that never ends.

"Damn good tickets," he'll say. "And the beer's free. And ice cold. How 'bout another?"

I will nod, because for once in my life there's no need to run anymore—from anything or to anywhere—and the beer will just appear in our mugs. And it'll be the best beer I've ever had. The Cards will win, too. Big.

Wrigley is riotous. My father wakes with a snort.

He looks around, unsure of where he is. When he sees me, he asks—as if it were thirty years ago—"Wanna beer?"

I look at him. He's so out of it.

"Fuck, boy. It's just a damn beer with your old man."

Or not.

Maybe I'm the one who's out of it.

My every action and decision over the last few decades have been so highly controlled that even a simple question stops me in my tracks.

I nod.

"Sure thing. I'll grab 'em."

Even in the last weeks of his life and even though he hasn't been to the grocery on his own in a couple of years, his fridge remains stocked with his favorite things: mayonnaise, wing-dings, whole milk, Oreos—which he likes cold—and lots of beer.

I laugh. Someone bought him Miller Lite.

"We ain't in Milwaukee," I say.

I dig around and there, in the back, are some bottles of Bud Light.

"Now we're talking."

I think of pouring mine into a glass, but know he'll throw me shit if I do, so I carry out two frosty Buds.

"Mike Shannon," he says with a laugh.

My dad loved the former St. Louis catcher turned long-time Cards announcer, who was raised in St. Louis and opened a successful steakhouse downtown. We ate at the restaurant once, and my father—happily buzzed—yelled at Shannon as he passed by, "I need a cold, frosty one!" a signature on-air and oft-used phrase by the beer-loving broadcaster. I was embarrassed, but Shannon appeared a few minutes later with a sudsy brew in a frosty glass.

"On the house!"

Mike Shannon was as golden as a beer in my father's eyes ever since.

I pop my dad's beer open, stick a straw into it and set it on the pullout tray in front of him. I pop mine, and he smiles at the sound.

"Cheers!"

"Cheers, boy!"

He leans over and takes a sip.

"Gotta use a goddamn straw to drink a beer now. What's the world comin' to?"

I take a sip. I haven't had a beer in years. I've forgotten how it tastes.

I'm a wine guy now, the mere utterance of which in the Ozarks could earn you a fist to the face or a bottle over the back of the head.

Over the years, especially as wine gained in popularity, I ate at nicer restaurants, met different friends and traveled more. I became an aficionado. I have tasted wine in Italy, Spain and the foot of Mt. Vesuvius, sipped champagne in Champagne, and had a bottle of Bordeaux to remember in Paris. I have become besties with a sommelier who has taught me the intricacies of growing grapes and aging wines, and who serves only the best wines. I enjoy a dry rosé on a warm summer evening. I enjoy a bold red on a cold winter's night.

My father believes I have become a snob.

"Beer is the drink of the real man," my dad would say. "Wine is the drink of the affected."

Maybe I am. Or maybe I have just expanded my horizons, literally and figuratively.

Or maybe, just maybe, I'm too uptight.

I drank a lot of beer in my life. Probably as much or more than my father.

In college, I would buy a case of beer for myself just to get a buzz. Twenty-four beers was simply a pregame. The man who worked at the liquor store close to campus knew me by name. He gave me discounts for buying in volume. The woman at the counter of the all-night convenience store a few blocks from our fraternity used to follow me around the store when I would enter inebriated, knowing my penchant for putting big-boy beers down my pants or microwaving burritos and eating them in the bathroom.

I nearly singlehandedly helped our fraternity win its first-ever Greek chug championship, an era-defining moment for a fraternity known more for its great grades, student leadership and community service than its partying. When my father came for parents' weekends, he would head straight for the kitchen, where a cold keg was waiting along with a mug in the cabinet with his name hand-painted on it by a little sister of the fraternity.

After college, I continued to party like it was 1999. I would buy kegs and stack the empties in my apartment. Red Solo cups were my wineglasses.

Before a baseball, football or hockey game, I would have to get a hundred dollars from the bank just so I could buy enough beer for myself.

And then one night after way too many beers, I placed a knife to my wrist and tried to end it all. I did a piss-poor job on myself, cutting the wrong way, not going deep enough. And while I was doing it, I thought in my stupor, "You selfish prick."

Why would I harm myself for something over which I had no control?

Why would I inflict even more pain on my mother?

Why would I commit such a selfish act that solved nothing but left a lifetime of damage?

I had close family members and friends who had died by suicide, and the domino effect of horror on those they loved continues to tumble forward to this day.

So I stopped. All the nonsense.

I stopped drinking cases of beer. I lost weight. I got up early and began to work out and write again.

And underneath all that pain and shame and weight, I discovered myself.

I stopped lying.

All the hiding and pretending to be someone else had left me a shell of who I was in my head. I had become a mannequin. An impostor. An actor.

My lines were "Please like me. Please love me. Please respect me. I'm just like you. No different."

But I didn't want to act anymore.

I vowed to do everything differently. I vowed to restart my life. I vowed to not live like my father.

My father ate like a "real man." And a real man drank whole milk, lots of beer and whiskey, and never a glass of water. A real man ate red meat every night, steaks rare, potatoes weighted down with melting butter and vegetables hidden in heavy cream sauces and cheese. Ice cream was homemade. When my dad went to the game, he ate everything from the concession stand: three hot dogs with mustard and onions, Dippin' Dots, pretzels, nachos, countless beers. I would get popcorn, and it would take everything for my father not to knock it out of my hands. There was no talk about gaining weight, or feeling hungover for work, or the health of your heart.

My father liked the old me better, even though it wasn't the authentic me.

I knew in my heart he didn't want me to change, because it might cause him to do so, as well.

Summer 2001

My parents arrived unexpectedly one day in St. Louis, as was their routine, meaning two days earlier than anticipated.

"Your parents are here," Gary said when he called me at work. "Do they not have calendars or understand how time works?"

"No," I said. "They live in their own world."

I arrived home to find my mother smoking on my front porch, wearing a bikini and telling a neighbor that she believed she was related to Suzanne Somers in a previous life. My father was shirtless in the porch swing, complaining that his chest hurt. They were set to fly on a vacation with my aunt and uncle.

My father wanted to go to a ball game, of course.

By that night, my father was having trouble catching his breath.

We called 911. My father was having a heart attack. When we arrived, the ER doctor said his artery was nearly blocked. He got a stent. The next day, he was hoping to still see a game and go on his trip.

He stayed with us the next week. Within a few days, I arrived home to find him drinking on the porch again, wholly unfazed by his near-death experience. He was eating a pizza and had gotten steaks for dinner.

"Listen, Stroke-y," I said to him. "Have you forgotten what just happened?"

"You stress about everything," he said. "You work too much. You worry too much."

"You're going to die, Dad, if you don't change," I said.

"We're all going to die, boy," he said. "No one gets outta this game alive."

The irony was rich, considering my dad had the Cards game on the TV, which he could hear through the living room windows. In fact, you could hear the game echo through my little city neighborhood, through open windows, from radios on people's porches, from the little bar that sat at the end of the street. My dad loved this most about where I lived: baseball wasn't just a game, it was a way of life.

I looked at him. He patted the porch swing as he did the couch.

"I need to go for a run and then prep for a morning meeting," I said.

"Sit a spell," he said. "Have a beer. Have some fun. You work too damn much."

I didn't really consider it. Every day I ran was a day I could erase when I never exercised. Every beer came with a question: How many calories are in that? A protein bar would be a much better option.

My father nodded.

He had nearly died and refused to change.

I focused on the second part of that sentence, not the first.

I changed into my running gear and put on my shoes as the game played. I took off down the sidewalk, charging away at my sub-7:30-a-minute pace, readying myself for an upcoming marathon, headed to the local park to do six miles.

At the corner of Lawn Avenue, I turned. My father was drinking a beer, rocking in the porch swing, listening to the game. The sun shone across his face, and he looked peaceful, happy, content.

I turned and continued to run. I was very good at running away.

October 2015

Now I just sit when I visit my father.

I do not run in the Ozarks. I'm scared of what might chase me.

Mostly, I'm just tired of running.

I have warily grown accustomed to the caregivers making the meals, cleaning the dishes and doing the laundry. It is not a comfortable thing for me to sit and have others do. I have never previously paid a dime for any of this in my life. We clean our own homes. We paint our own houses. We wash our own cars. The only thing I've allowed is a lawn company to mow our large yard in Michigan. My work schedule—sunup to sundown like an Ozarks farmer—exhausts me. It's worth it to pay for a few things, I've learned.

My father's head would explode if he knew how much the home care company charged each month. He would burst into their offices and scream, "You are rippin' me off!"

It's the ultimate irony that my father never spent his money on anything he could enjoy while he was healthy.

Now he spends every dime to have someone clean him and watch him die.

A couple of years ago, I received notification that I was back in my father's trust.

"I trust you," he told me. "Not only with my money but also my life. Always have. You just needed to be tested a little."

I had not only been designated with helping to make all of his financial decisions but I had also been listed as his medical power of attorney. I spend his money now to care for him at home. I pamper him, as I did my mom, with things he never utilized, like air-conditioning and a big TV. I will honor his last and most important request, even if it requires me to chip in my own money to do so. We all deserve the dignity of dying at home.

My dad is sleeping again, his head lolled to one side, his chipmunk cheeks sagging like storm clouds.

The old car has run out of gas. The keg is empty. The game nearly over.

My father stomped into his seventies with his pounding gait, beer in hand, a stent in his heart, a touch of dementia and a spirit as loaded as the shotgun he kept under his bed.

I marched into my forties with a bad back, aching knees, rotator cuff issues, carpal tunnel and 20-400 vision.

My father retired at fifty-five.

I never see myself retiring.

Who is the truly healthy one here?

My father's philosophy was to work as hard as you partied. The difference was you should party more than you work. When work was over, it was over.

I've chosen a career that never ends. Being an author has no clock attached to it, no normal work schedule, no nine to five, workin' for the weekend.

I go morning, noon and night. Write, edit, speeches, book clubs, social media, appearances. Saturdays are Mondays.

My father's bloated belly rises and falls. The bill of his Cards cap throws a shadow over his face.

I want to be active and healthy at ninety, but is that guaranteed, no matter how well I take care of myself?

None of us gets out of this game alive, boy.

My father has nearly sliced off a finger with a chainsaw, almost whacked off his hand with a table saw, fallen off the roof trying to clean the gutters and tumbled down a bluff at the old cabin fixing the posts on the deck.

"I'm up!" he'd yell, hands over his head, blood gushing. "All good!"

He would grab a beer or something stronger, drink away the pain and go on as if nothing had ever happened.

A scrapbook on a side table catches my eye, and I grab it as quietly as possible.

It's an old leather-bound scrapbook. Embossed on the cover is Family Photos.

I placed it here on purpose.

I wanted my dad to be surrounded by photos of family. I instructed the caregivers to pick it up on occasion and show him pictures.

I open it. The thick, black construction paper crumbles as I turn the pages. It is collapsing with age. The four corners that long held the photos in place on the page are cockeyed or missing. Many photos have fallen into the spine.

I look at the pages. Much work was taken to position the photos just so: which ones would look best angled, which ones should be edited out, which ones should follow the other to tell the perfect story.

All of these mementoes of my family's past are relics now: the scrapbooks and Polaroids, the holiday cards and handwritten letters, the recipe cards and pressed flowers— Queen Anne's lace and roses.

I used to roll my eyes when my father would say the world was changing too quickly and forgetting the things that were important.

So I would buy him an answering machine, a laptop, a cell phone. I taught him how to text and take photos with his phone.

I look at the scrapbook.

Where do I—where do we—keep our collective memories now?

Facebook? Instagram? TikTok?

These often aren't real memories; they're curated moments for people we don't know.

Will we have scrapbooks when today's teens are my father's age? Will they have a handwritten letter from a loved one to remind them of that person, what they meant, how they tilted their *T*s or curled their *Q*s, like you still do? Or will all of that be deleted over the years, gone with a click, the road to our pasts erased?

I flip through the pages of the scrapbook as if it were a Rolodex—yet another relic—of my family's history.

My father as a baby.

My grandparents holding him.

My father eating that ice cream cone as a kid.

My father's senior high school photo.

My father's fraternity photo.

My father in the National Guard.

My dad and mom getting married.

Having Todd.

Holding me.

The old cabin.

The family fishing.

The family aging.

My father with a Cards hat on his head and a beer in his hand.

Ditto.

Ditto.

Photos at Cardinal games.

My mom and dad on vacation.

My mom and dad at the cabin.

My dad asleep on the couch after Thanksgiving.

I glance over at him.

So much has changed. So little has.

A photo falls free and lands on my lap.

It's an old Polaroid of me and my brother at Silver Dollar City, the 1880s-style theme park in Branson, Missouri. We used to go there as a family. We loved the rides, especially Fire in the Hole, but my father most enjoyed watching the resident craftsmen demonstrate heritage crafts. There were blacksmiths, candle and candy makers, potters, glassblowers and lye soap craftsmen—all in old-timey costumes—demonstrating lost American crafts.

In the old photo, I am maybe five and watching a craftsman work. My fists are wedged into the sides of my waist. Even as a kid, I was already standing like my father. I flip through the album again. I am standing just like him. And I still do.

I thumb through it again, quickly.

There is my father, his life passing before my eyes in flashes, as quickly as it must have gone by to him.

I remember my father throwing a baseball to me as a kid. I remember all the games I attended with my dad. I think of my father being tested for dementia and being unable to draw a baseball diamond.

Blink of God's eye, my mom whispers to me.

At the end of the scrapbook, there is a photo of my friends and me—my father with a beer in hand—tailgating before a Cards game.

One of my best friends told me that day I've been driven so long in life that I don't even know who's driving any more.

"You need to be more like your dad," he said.

That infuriated me.

But now I see that my father is going to walk into heaven drunk off his ass, slap God so hard on the back that he'll knock Him off his winged feet and ask Him if the angelic happy hour is free.

"Fuck the harps!" he'll scream. "Put on some Helen Reddy! And I need more Tabasco in my Bloody Mary!"

God, my dad is fun.

A royal pain in the ass but crown-of-thorns fun.

I hate being so rigid.

But I had to be in order to get this far.

Didn't I?

I glance at that photo of me from so long ago standing like my dad.

From a distance, Gary used to say he had trouble distinguishing me from my father.

"You walk the same," he'd say. "You stand the same. But it's different, too."

"How?" I would ask, never seeing it.

"You stand as if you're about to take on the world," Gary said. "But your father looks as if he's about to slap it on the ass and hand it a drink."

I see it now. Same stance. Different perspective.

And that's when it hits me: perhaps it's me who was a little bit jealous of how easy his life started out.

He was cute. He was fun. He was smart. He could play baseball and tennis. He could fit in, drink beer and laugh without any guilt, without fearing any slipup, without worrying people might think, *What's wrong with this guy?* His successful career came easy. A game of golf, a dirty joke, a meeting over a martini.

Me? I had to hide. I had to be a chameleon. I had to adapt.

I had to stand with my hands on my waist, shoulders back, ready to go.

Maybe forging through all that hard stuff made me who I am.

And maybe when it got too hard for my dad—a challenging wife, the loss of a son, another son who never fit in—he just wanted it all to be easy again.

It must have been hard to adapt to a world that constantly was changing. I try to put myself in his shoes; a man unable to run but who can deftly avoid confronting reality.

I watch him sleep.

How many times did he watch me sleep?

Did he ever whisper to me, "Be strong, son"?

Did he ever coo to me, "I love you"?

And did he do it when I was too young to comprehend it, only when he was comfortable saying it, and even though I don't remember it, did he say it so many times to me back then that his words stuck in me and grew in the oddest of ways, like when a sycamore grows at a forty-five-degree angle from the side of a bank over a creek? The rushing water tries for decades to wash it away, but it holds tough, still growing and reaching for the light, even though it doesn't do it quite like everyone else.

Why didn't I tell him I loved him when I had the chance? Why didn't we stand next to each other, hands on hips, and say it?

Maybe it *was* easy, and I'm culpable in this whole mess, too. Maybe I helped make it too damn hard, as well. Maybe he just wanted it to be simple again, for a brief moment in his life, so that he could forget about everything.

We all make life too damn hard. We overthink. We judge. We are judged. We hate. But sometimes we just have to be in the flow of the game, learn how to take a pitch, decide whether we want to bunt or hit for the bleachers. Sometimes it's okay to sit a spell and watch the action.

My dad wakes with a snort, looks over at me, and I swear I can see his face light up.

I'm still here, Dad, I think.

He watches me watching him.

I can hear him say, "You know, boy, sometimes all I wanted was for my son to sit down for a second and have a beer with his old man."

Tears well in my eyes, but he's too sleepy to see that.

I pick up my can and polish it off.

"I think I'll have another one if that's okay by you," I say.

He smiles. "I'd like that."

"Me, too."

I return just in time to see Piscotty strike out. The Cubs faithful go bonkers.

My father looks at me, confused.

"Cards lost, Dad," I say. "I'm so sorry."

"I knew it." His face morphs to disgust as he watches Wrigley rock.

"It was Chicago's time," I say. "Good for them."

"Good for them?" he asks. "Don't be soft, boy."

I am soft. I'm a marshmallow buried under Ozarks red clay.

It's a mob scene at Wrigley.

"Turn it off!" he yells. "We lost!" he says again.

"No," I say, drinking my beer. "We won."

"How you figure that, boy," he says.

"Team went farther than we expected. Exceeded a lot of expectations. Made a lot of memories."

He shakes his head for the longest time at me. But at the end, he nods.

"Good season," he says.

I raise my beer to his optimism.

"And there's always next year," I say.

The words float in the air. My father doesn't say a word. He just continues to stare at me. He blinks. I see a tear.

"Lots of good seasons," he says.

"More wins than losses, right, Dad?"

"Damn right."

I finish my beer, and my father grows sleepy. I make him some soup. He eats it slowly and then he yawns.

"Wanna help me to bed?" he asks, even though it's still early.

I wheel him to the bathroom and begin to brush his teeth and wash him.

His skin is no longer skin. It is onion paper. His hands and arms are mottled purple. If you grab him too hard by the arm or try to catch him as he's about to fall, his skin just sloughs off, like the scales on the fish he used to clean alongside the creek.

I wash his face. I gingerly wash his arms. I wash his legs. I rub lotion onto his sloped back, now arched like the one in St. Louis. I dust baby power so he won't get a rash. I put moisturizer on his face, something he's never done in his life.

These are acts of love.

Aren't they?

Only with this man do I have to ask myself this question.

Gary taught me to hug. "You don't even hug right," he said when we met. I wouldn't grasp tightly, hug back. I would just stand there, an alien being taught affection.

I would always be the first to let go. But Gary would just hold me until I had no other choice but to hug back, until I could feel him, not just his body, but his entire soul radiating into mine. After a while, I began to hold him for so long that I felt the world dissolve around me. I held him so long that I was scared to let go or I wouldn't be able to stand on my own when I did.

Touching. Hugging. Caressing. Saying kind words. These acts do not make a real man or a real woman. They do not make someone less real. They simply make us human.

I rub more lotion on my dad's back. His body becomes rigid. I do not stop. Finally, his shoulders soften. He sighs like my dogs do when they get a bath, and I towel them dry and brush their coats. I keep rubbing and caressing and touching. I move to get my father's favorite Cardinals sweatshirt. He gets chilly even if it's a hundred degrees outside. I am just like him.

"Don't stop," he says.

I turn and look at him.

"Okay, Dad," I say.

I grab the lotion and massage it into his shoulders.

I help him into bed. It takes two people to do that now, but somehow I lift him into bed all on my own.

Outside, the whip-poor-wills call, over and over.

Whip-poor-will. Whip-poor-will. Whip-poor-will.

My dad cocks his head. He smiles.

"Your mom always said them birds singin' meant an Ozarks day had come to an end."

"She was a wise woman," I say.

He nods.

I also think of the other legend my mother used to always share: whip-poor-wills singing near a house were an omen of death.

"Don't call back at night," she would tell me. "It's an invitation. If someone returns its whistle, and the bird stops calling, the person who answers will die."

I cannot shake this memory, so I walk over and crack his bedroom window even though it's a tad chilly.

A squirrel dashes up a tree with an acorn. A chipmunk watches me from a stump. A cardinal—irony of ironies—alights in a bush.

I close my eyes for a second, remembering a chipmunk that was hit by a car while I was running along the lakeshore a few weeks ago. It had tried to scamper across the road, thinking all was safe, when a car went barreling down the quiet lane much too fast. Another chipmunk came running out from the woods and stood over its companion. Whether the grieving was its mother, brother, sister, wife, husband, friend, I do not know, but it screamed like you or I would when someone we love passes unexpectedly. I grabbed a branch and a large piece of tree bark and moved the chipmunk into the woods. I grabbed a stick, dug a hole in the muddy ground, buried it and created a makeshift cross out of twigs. When I was done, the grieving chipmunk looked at me, its little hands in front of its face as if it were praying. It screamed again before laying directly atop the grave.

Being a runner has not only brought me closer to life, it has brought me closer to death. I've witnessed squirrels, deer, birds die out in the middle of nowhere, as if death were waiting until I arrived alone. As if I were meant to be the one to be with them at the end.

I hear my mother's voice again.

She told me after my grandmother's death that some people are spirit guides for the dead. Not in an evil way, but in a good way. She told me that the dying often know death is imminent, and they wait for the right person to be with them to cross over because they know they will be surrounded by positive energy, love and light, and they die knowing they are not alone, which is one of our greatest gifts when we leave this world.

"We know not exactly what lies ahead of us," my mom said, "which can cause tremendous anxiety, but we know what is directly beside us, and that can provide not only love and calm but also a guide into the next chapter. We are those spirits for the dead, you and me, Wade. We will always be there for the dead. Don't run from it. Embrace it."

My mom died with only me in the room beside her.

You understand great loss when you're the only one left sitting at your family's dining room table and all of the other chairs are empty. I am alone, and I am not alone. I have Gary, I have family, I have friends. But those people who knew me before anyone else in this world, the ones who hugged me, loved me, hurt me, helped me, raised me and knocked me back down are soon all to be gone. There will be no Rouse left standing in line in front of me. I am the next to go, and I am okay with that. I tell Gary I know for certain that I will die first, and I'm pretty certain I will. I don't tell him that to hurt him, nor do I expect or want the rest of my life to be a short one. I want a long life, filled with great joy, travel, work and love. But I cannot bury another. I cannot say goodbye to Gary without saying goodbye to myself. I have been strong many times in my life. I don't want to be strong anymore. I've been a spirit guide long enough.

I watch the critters scamper around in the yard, then I tuck my dad into bed and head to the door.

I turn off the light.

"Good night, Dad."

"Boy?"

"Yeah."

"Sit a spell longer."

I take a seat on the edge of his bed and reach for his hand.

Whip-poor-will. Whip-poor-will. Whip-poor-will.

He turns his head toward the window and smiles. He closes his eyes.

And then he reaches back and puts his hand on mine, and the entire world falls away.

It's not just the end of another day, another game, another season.

It's the end.

I know it.

My dad knows it, too.

"I'm so tired, boy," he says. "Dog tired."

"I know," I say. "It's okay, Dad. It's okay to be tired. It's okay to let go. You had a good run."

"Like the Cards?"

"Better than that," I say.

"What do you think about next season?" he asks.

"Well, I think it's going to be tough," I say. "Won't be

the same." I stop and look at him, right in the eyes. "It won't ever be the same."

He looks at me.

"I do love ya, boy. You need to know that."

My soul stills. For just a moment. After fifty years.

I can hear the crowd—my mom, my family, my ghosts—cheer wildly at the result.

A walk-off home run in the bottom of the ninth!

My father grips my hand. "You're my *next* season. Always remember that."

I don't want to cry, but I do. I sob. I lean in and my father holds me, maybe for the first—and last—time in our lives.

"You're gonna be alright, boy," he whispers, his voice strong. "'Cause I taught you to be tough, didn't I?"

I don't want to let go. For once, he doesn't either.

"You sure did, Dad."

Whip-poor-will. Whip-poor-will. Whip-poor-will.

"I think she's a-callin' me home," he says.

Whip-poor-will. Whip-poor-will. Whip-poor-will.

All of a sudden, my dad musters the energy to purse his lips and whistle back, just like he used to do when he was young. He was the master of any birdcall, be it a bobwhite or loon, gobble or hoot. But I'd forgotten he was best at mimicking a whip-poor-will.

I lift my head and clamp my eyes shut, waiting for the bird to answer.

The stadium goes quiet.

BOTTOM OF THE 9TH

"Extra Innings"

Spring 2019

I stop after a long run in Forest Park to get a drink from the fountain. I am back in St. Louis, in my old stomping grounds, on a book tour. I have visited friends and seen the Cardinals' new Ballpark Village.

Forest Park, the setting for the 1904 World's Fair and considered the heart of St. Louis, was the place I trained for my first marathon. 6.2 miles around the park. Four times around was nearly a marathon. It was the place I learned to run. At first I was just running away from the past. Then, one day, I realized I was running with conviction, a purpose, a goal, just like Lou Brock stealing second base. I was making my way home. I just didn't know it yet.

It is a windy, semi-warm spring day where the clouds bounce along the sky like a grounder up the middle. I am listening to a Cardinals game, and that's when it hits me. My father did show up for my marathon. He came with my mom and rooted me on the whole way. He had a beer in hand for me when the race was over. He was wearing a

Cards hat that he took off and waved as I crossed the finish line.

My dad may have never been there enough for me when
I was a kid, but he did show up.

He was there at the end.

We ran a marathon, my father and I.

I stop and get a big drink from a water fountain, pausing
to watch a father play catch with his son. The man and boy
both look very young—something I feel about everyone
now that I'm firmly entrenched in my fifties. The father is
giving his son pointers on how to hold his glove, not to take
his eye off the ball, how to set himself before he throws.
The father is gentle, reassuring, and the son listens to him.

I turn and get another drink from the fountain, and when
I look back, the boy's glove is off and he has dissolved into
tears. The dad kneels down and talks to his son, and, within
a minute or so, they are playing catch again.

That's the thing about baseball, I think as I watch them, the
sound of the ball hitting the leather as comforting a sound
as the spring wind. *It's a game. It's supposed to be fun.*

Like life.

"Wanna play?"

For a second, I don't know they are talking to me. I remove my earbuds.

"Got another glove," the father yells. "Would be good for
him to learn some pointers from a guy who's not his father."

The dad laughs, as do I. *What could I teach a kid about
baseball?* I think. *I never played really. Haven't played in forever.
I'm just a fan of the game.*

I nearly say no, but something makes me jog over and take the glove.

"Noticed you wearing a Cards cap," the father says. "We're big fans."

"My dad's taken me to three games my whole life!" the kid says excitedly, forgetting he was just upset, holding up his free hand to show three fingers. "How many games have you been to?"

"Too many to count," I say.

"Wow!" the kid says.

"What was your favorite game you ever went to?" I ask.

He looks at me and then his father. "All of them," he says. "'Cause I went with my dad." He stops. "What was your favorite?"

I stare at the kid, all rosy cheeks and freckles and acres of life ahead of him.

"Game 4. Cards-Cubs," I say. "2015."

The father gives me an odd look and tilts his head. "But they lost, right?" he asks. "To the Cubs! Gave them a post-season series for the first time ever in Wrigley Field. How could that be your favorite?"

The boy scrunches up his face as if he's just eaten a handful of Sour Patch Kids. "Yeah! How?"

For a moment, I shut my eyes, not to consider his question really but to stop my tears. When I open them, the world is bright.

"Because I went with my dad, too."

★ ★ ★ ★ ★

Acknowledgments

I have never been the type of memoirist who sets out to write a "revenge" or a "blame" book. My memoirs always are an attempt to understand better not only myself but also those around me. My memoirs are an attempt to answer the big questions in life that haunt and daunt me and ones I believe do the same to you. At the top of the list for so many of us sit our relationships with our parents and our children. After my mother's death and as I slid into my fifties, my big questions were, Will I ever have closure with my father? And why does that matter so much to me? Despite everything, I believed my father loved me but had little capacity to show it. But—and this is a big *but*—did he like me? Moreover, did I become the man I am today *because of* my father or *in spite of* my father?

Many of the stories about my father that I share in *Magic Season* are stories my dad would happily tell a Walmart greeter. But some of the memories I share are painful. I must say this because it's important to me: I would never try to hurt my dad. My goal is to honor him by understanding him. All of us are flawed souls. No one is perfect. And I believe that love, understanding and forgiveness only come when we are able take those we love—especially our parents—off a pedestal, put them on the ground, stare them in the eyes and see them as we see ourselves: as imperfect people who are just trying their damndest most days to do the best they can. I also believe in Anne Lamott's advice in *Bird by Bird* (with an asterisk): "You own everything that happened to you. Tell your stories. If people wanted you to write warmly about them, they should have behaved better." My asterisk: But try hard to understand them, too. I did my darndest, dad, to keep honor and honesty equal on memoir's playing field.

When I was a little boy, I would watch the faces of my grandmothers and my mother when they read Erma Bombeck's column, At Wit's End, in our local paper. After they'd had a long day or week of work, their faces would relax as they read, then lift, their mouths would turn up and laughter would pour forth. I began to read Erma, and as I grew up, I remembered her and thought, "If I could do that... If I could make people stop, if I could make people think, if I could make people laugh, if I could change them with my words and my life, that would be a dream come true."

My career as an author began in 2006 with the publication of my first memoir, *America's Boy*. I wrote three subsequent memoirs, all humorous, all poignant, before launching into fiction. I've now written ten novels under the pen name Viola Shipman, which I chose to honor my working poor Ozarks grandma, whose memory and sac-rifices inspire my fiction.

I'm beyond humbled to return to writing nonfiction again. My dream has, once again, come true.

It has been a long journey, personally and professionally, to be here a decade after my last memoir was published. I think I needed time to heal, to reflect, to laugh, and to cry (a lot) before writing this memoir and treading into the oh-so-nightmarishly-painful but oh-so-cathartic world of nonfiction again.

I must first thank my husband, Gary, who—nearly twenty years ago now when I was at another personal and professional crossroads—said, "Just write a book," when I said I wanted to write a book. "Let's go on an adventure together." And when I completed half of that first book as fiction, he read it and said, "This sounds nothing like you. Write another book." So I did. And it's been his love, sup-port, childlike optimism and blunt honesty that have kept our adventure going for twenty-five years of marriage and my sixteen years as an author. He had no idea, between my career, insanity and family, what he was signing up for. I love you.

When I was searching for the next memoir to write, one of my best friends from college told me, "Dude, you are completely overlooking the book you were born to write: the one about you and your old man. It won't be easy, but it might help a lot of people...including you. Don't be a lame-ass. Write it." So, Matt Bradley, thank you for giv-ing me this kernel of an idea long ago in your inimitable way. Next beer's on me.

My agent, Wendy Sherman, has been with me from day one. She sold my first memoir in 2005. Over the last nearly two decades, she has championed, cheered, listened to, loved, supported, sold and nurtured not only my career but me. That is what you look for in a literary agent: someone who is not only a great agent but an even greater person. She is. My career has moved from memoir to fiction and now—my dream—to both genres. I can't wait to see what the next two decades bring.

I remember when Wendy emailed me and said, "I met this editor for lunch I think you'd love. I feel you two are going to hit it off." Was she ever right. My editor, John Glynn, loved *Magic Season* when it was untitled and just a few pages long. He believed in the story of family and forgiveness I wanted to tell—a story without blame and filled with hope—and that empowered me to write the memoir I wanted. Incidentally, I had just read John's memoir, *Out East*, before we officially met. It seemed as if this was predestined. And I believe that it was. The hardest part of our working relationship has been the constant stroking of John's ego, considering his lack of self-confidence regarding his appearance and talent. I'm here for you, John.

Thank you to Hanover Square Press and Peter Joseph. It's an honor to be a part of your imprint and vision. I feel, ever since my days with the inimitable Tom Dunne, we were meant to work together again.

Huge, heartfelt thanks to Kathleen Carter, who is not only a superbly talented publicist but also an incredible person. I can never thank her enough for her belief, support, expertise and tireless dedication.

If you see my books out in the wild, thank Randy Chan. I do all the time.

Thanks to Carol Fitzgerald and her team at The Book Report Network. Carol is a mentor and friend and keeps me uplifted and on track.

Thank you to Meg Walker for all her creative marketing and kindness.

And ditto to Danielle Noe, whose behind-the-scenes efforts have made a huge difference in my career.

My father, Ted, was one of a kind. "God broke the mold when He made me, boy," he used to tell me. "No, Dad. He broke the mold on purpose," I used to reply. There will never be another like my dad. Despite our complicated history, I loved him and always will. And the couch will always seem empty without him. But I know he's waiting for me with a frosty-cold beer, a fluffy cloud and a Cards game that never ends.

As I write these acknowledgments, the St. Louis Cardinals had won seventeen consecutive games to secure a 2021 playoff spot. They were dead in the water over the summer, suffering heart-wrenching losses that seemed to gut the team. And yet I continued to watch. When they began to win, my kernel of hope grew into a tree of belief. They lost in the bottom of the ninth to the Dodgers in the Wild Card game, a heartbreaking end to a valiant season. But their run sums up why I love the game, why I love the Cardinals and why I will always believe that a miracle—a "magic season"—can occur at any moment…if you don't give up. You have to see the best in yourself and your team, lift one another when you need it most. Right, Dad?

I truly hope you love *Magic Season*. And I hope, when you're finished, you might say about the book and even more about life—as Jack Buck did when the Cards would come out on top—"And that's a winner, folks!"